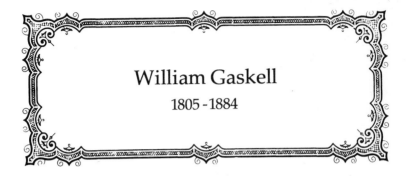

William Gaskell

1805 - 1884

1. William Gaskell by W. Percy, 1872.

WILLIAM GASKELL
1805 - 1884

A PORTRAIT BY
Barbara Brill

1984

Manchester Literary and

Philosophical Publications Ltd

© 1984 Barbara Brill
First published 1984
by Manchester Literary and Philosophical Publications Ltd
55 Brown Street, Manchester
Designed and produced by
Janet Allan
Printed in Great Britain by
Manchester Free Press
59 Whitworth Street, Manchester

ISBN No 0 902428 05 5

British Library Cataloguing in Publication Data

Brill, Barbara
    William Gaskell
    1805-1884
    1. Gaskell, William 2. Unitarians—England—biography
    1. Title
    288'. 092'4 BX 9869. 93/

iv

Contents

ILLUSTRATIONS

Endpapers
front: Manchester in 1828 (the year William Gaskell was
appointed to Cross Street Chapel) Bancks & Co.
back: Manchester in 1884 (the year of his death) Bacon.

Our thanks are due to the following for permission to reproduce
the illustrations: Cross Street Chapel for numbers 17, 22, 23, 26,
30, 34, 38 and 40. Professor Chapple, 16. Cheshire Life, 13.
Manchester City Art Gallery, 36. Manchester College Oxford, 9.
Manchester Lit & Phil, 12, 18, 27. Manchester Public Libraries,
11, 24, 32, 37. Chris Makepeace, 19, 20, 21, 28, 29. Glasgow
University, 7, 8. Mrs Trevor Jones, 15. National Portrait Gallery,
14. Newcastle Literary and Philosophical Society, 10. Portico
Library, 35, 41. John Rylands Library, 31. Unitarian College,
Manchester, 1, 42. Warrington Public Library, 2-6. We would
also like to acknowledge help with photography from Montage,
Design and Photography from Alastair Hamilton and from Ian
Summers who photographed numbers 1-6, 26, 35 and 39.
Number 15 is from a photograph by Stanley Travers.

Foreword

The pleasure I feel in introducing Mrs Barbara Brill's book has been greatly enhanced by the fact that I have been privileged to watch it grow from its first tentative beginnings through its successive stages to its present form. It is the first book to be written primarily about William Gaskell, known to most readers only as the husband of Elizabeth and overshadowed by her fame as a novelist. It had long been Mrs Brill's conviction that William deserved a book not, of course, 'all to himself'—the lives of husband and wife were far too deeply interfused for that—but at least focussed upon him as a significant figure in his own right. Accordingly her book must be regarded as a pioneer work breaking new ground although, with characteristic modesty, its author prefers to think of it as 'work in progress' which may prompt others to undertake further researches in this less familiar field.

The question Barbara Brill had to ask herself at the outset was to what kind of readership her book should be addressed, whether to Gaskell specialists or to a wider public. I believe she has successfully met both requirements by giving us a book which is at one popular and scholarly and therefore likely to appeal to both categories of readers. She has achieved this by assembling the facts she has discovered about William Gaskell and then appending to each section of her book in its proper chronological place the relevant historical and bibliographical material which gives her work the backing of sound scholarship.

One of the principal satisfactions of my ministry at Cross Street Chapel has been the re-discovery of its historical dimension. I have not been alone in this enterprise. It has been shared by Mr Harry Hewerdine, for many years Chairman of the Congregation, and his son John who has put his expertise as a photographer at our service: by Mr Lester Burney to whom we owe two valuable books on the Chapel, its School and its College: Dr Lionel Angus-Butterworth of Buxton whose forebears were members and benefactors of the Chapel from its earliest days: by research students of the Universities of Manchester and Cambridge; by John Seed who knows more about Unitarianism than most Unitarians do: and by Mrs Mary Thwaite of Goostrey and Dr Monica Frykstedt of the University of Uppsala, who, while preparing her Doctoral Dissertation, discovered a valuable source in the Chapel's complete collection of the Reports of the Ministry to the Poor inaugurated in 1833 and continuing through the Gaskell period and beyond. To the researches of this congenial confraternity Barbara Brill, in the book I have the honour to introduce, has made an important and original contribution.

E.J. Raymond Cook,
Minister of Cross Street Chapel

Acknowledgements

The length of the list which follows is a measure of the amount of help I have received at every stage in the preparation of this book and an acknowledgement of the gratitude I owe to those who have given it. I am particularly indebted to Rev E.J.R. Cook, M.A., B.D without whose support the book would never have been written and who drew it to the attention of the publishers, the Manchester Literary and Philosophical Society; Rev James McClelland, M.A., Secretary of the Hibbert Trust, and the administrators of the Trust for generous financial backing; Rev Andrew Hill, B.A., A.L.A. of Edinburgh for reading the manuscript and making valuable suggestions; Rev A.J. Long, M.A., Principal of the Unitarian College Manchester for ready offers of help with research; Mrs Janet Allan of the Portico Library who has taken a keen personal interest in the book from the beginning, guided its progress throughout with enthusiasm and drive, and at the end cheerfully assumed the onerous responsibility of preparing it for publication; Mr Harry Hewerdine for willing help with Cross Street Chapel history; Mr J. Geoffrey Sharps of Scarborough for advice and for supplying research material relating to the home life and family background of the Gaskells; Mrs Mary Thwaite of Goostrey for providing details of the Gaskell Collection at Brook Street Chapel, Knutsford; Dr William Brockbank for allowing me access to the Unitarian College Collection in the John Rylands University Library and Mr Ian Summers for taking special photographs. The following Libraries and Colleges have given valuable assistance: Warrington Central Library (Mr D.A. Rogers); John Rylands University Library (Miss Glenise

Mathieson); Manchester Central Library, Language and Literature Library (Miss Christine Lingard); Manchester College, Oxford (Mrs Barbara Smith); the University of Glasgow (Archives Department); The International Society, Manchester (Mrs Christine Hayes and Miss Eileen Walsh). The following individuals have helped me to fill in missing details: Mrs Trevor Jones (family history); Dr Guest-Gornall (Samuel Gaskell); Mr Alfred Burgess (John Harland's Annals), and many others have shown interest and proferred help, Mrs Catherine Powers has patiently and painstakingly typed the manuscript.

Barbara Brill

Introduction

William Gaskell lived through a period of immense change. Born in Warrington at the beginning of the nineteenth century he spent most of his seventy-nine years in Manchester, which like other rapidly spreading industrial towns was facing the bewildering problems created by the Industrial Revolution. In his lifetime he saw the solving of many of these problems by the shaping of new laws to improve living and working conditions in the overcrowded city, largely brought about through the spread of humanitarian views. As a clergyman William Gaskell played an important part in the spreading of these views.

Although a fine preacher attracting large congregations William did not consider this his most important role. He came down from the pulpit and out of the chapel to move among and talk on equal terms with all types and classes of men and women, the prosperous and the poor, the cultured and the uneducated. As a Unitarian he rated education highly and devoted much of his time to teaching and lecturing at colleges and working men's clubs, and also took a number of private pupils under his wing. He was born at a time when Unitarians had to face charges from the Established Church of holding anti-Christian opinions, but the Reverend William Gaskell lived to see the acceptance and spread of their beliefs. His personal influence and example contributed largely to this change of attitude.

William lived in harmony with his wife Elizabeth, the famous novelist and their four daughters, making their home in the heart of Manchester a welcoming meeting place for friends and a haven for those in trouble. Wherever he stands in chapel, college, committee room or home William Gaskell is seen as a

1

man of stability at a time of shifting values, and a radiating focus of goodwill.

Much has been written about Mrs Gaskell and her letters reveal her personality and bring alive for us the atmosphere of the Gaskell home and her husband's busy life, with some intimate sidelights on his character. Neither she nor William kept the letters they exchanged with each other. Elizabeth died nearly twenty years before her husband and he never kept any private letters so his life as a widower can only be guessed at but there is evidence in plenty of his continuing public work.

This book written to mark the hundredth anniversary of his death is an attempt to gather together all I have learnt from William Gaskell's contribution to the times in which he lived and through his work it is hoped we may glimpse the man.

CHAPTER 1

Early Influences

Warrington was already beginning to hum with the sound of industrial changes when William Gaskell was born there in 1805. The Sankey Canal had been supplying the town with coal from St Helens for fifty years and the first steam engine to be used in the Lancashire cotton industry was installed at a mill in Warrington in 1787. In that year its population was 9,000 and by the time William had reached manhood it had increased to 13,600. It is a town with origins going back to the Bronze Age, owing its existence to its position on the River Mersey and the lives of its townspeople have been influenced by this important waterway.

By the sixteenth century Warrington had become a busy trade centre, its bridge across the Mersey providing the main route from the south to the north-west and large vessels could proceed from Liverpool as far as the town, from which goods could be carried on by barge to Manchester. Its earliest industries were copper-smelting and weaving, and during the eighteenth century the manufacture of coarse sailcloth was introduced, bringing wealth to the town as it supplied much of the heavy sailcloth required by the Navy. The cloth was made from hemp and flax brought from Russia to Liverpool and then by river to Warrington.

This was the trade in which the Gaskell family was engaged at the time of William's birth, his father, also William, having a thriving business in Buttermarket Street. William Gaskell senior was married to Margaret Jackson, also of Warrington, and their first home was in Latchford, then a fashionable suburb of Warrington that boasted one of the first Sunday Schools in England, inaugurated at St James' Church in 1779, and here too

3

was the cotton mill powered by a Boulton & Watt steam engine. Here William was born on 24 July 1805, the eldest of six children, the only one whose birth is recorded in the chapel register as being at Latchford, his brothers and sisters being at Warrington. This chapel was the Sankey Street Unitarian Chapel where many other Gaskell births had been registered, for the Warrington branch of the family had a long and close association with this Dissenting chapel. The building now named Cairo Street Chapel is still standing, one of the oldest surviving places of worship in the town and was built in 1745 on the site of an earlier chapel where one Roger Gaskell, maltster, had registered the birth of his son John in 1724. The Gaskell family through their links with the Chapel were receptive to the ideas that emanated from Warrington Academy, founded by John Seddon, one of the ministers of Sankey Street Chapel fifty years before William's birth. The Academy came to be spoken of as the cradle of Unitarianism.

2. The Sankey Street Chapel, Warrington, from the south east. Sketch by Robert Booth c 1830.

Because William was raised in this atmosphere and absorbed the Unitarian beliefs that were to guide him throughout life it is important to take a look at the development of Unitarianism and to assess its standing at the time of his birth. These are some of the stages in its history up until that time. As early as the fourth century Arius of the Church of Alexandria had questioned the idea of God the Father, God the Son. His followers believed that Father and Son were distinct and Christ though divine was not equal to God. Although this was declared a heresy in AD325 these Arian beliefs continued to be held and were expressed with vigour over a thousand years later by the Italian Faustus Socinus (1539-1604). His ideas were ripe for discussion in England during the dissensions in the Church that followed the Reformation. The Socinians went further than the Arians casting doubts on the divinity of Christ, basing their belief on a close investigation of the New Testament and the application of reason to its interpretation.

3. The River Mersey at Patten's and Lyon's Quay, Warrington. Sketch by Robert Booth c 1830.

In England it was John Locke (1632-1704) who propounded the same theories advocating wider studies of natural laws alongside the Scriptures in the search for truth. He was spoken of as the Socinus of his age. During his lifetime the first of the nonconformist academies was established to provide for the education of lay and divinity students from among Dissenters who at that time in England were denied the opportunity of a university education. Warrington Academy was one of these establishments where a broadly-based education fitted men for other professions as well as the ministry.

Locke's life spanned the period of fluctuating attitudes towards nonconformists. During the Commonwealth period an attempt to impose a Scottish-type Presbyterian system failed, but it was a time when the country came near to an established Independency. Then followed the restoration of Charles II and the passing of the Act of Uniformity, under which only persons episcopally ordained could hold office in the Church of England, and which required that all incumbents should use the Book of Common Prayer. Dissenters began to meet secretly but this was made illegal by the Conventicle Act of 1664 that limited meetings for worship to members of the family and five others. On the accession of William and Mary the Act of Toleration granted a measure of freedom to nonconformists, giving them the right to erect their own meeting places and to choose their own form of service; but this Act did not grant them freedom of doctrine, as they had to conform to the Thirty-nine Articles of the Church of England, and Roman Catholics and Anti-Trinitarians were specifically excluded.

In 1719 at a meeting of Dissenting ministers at the Salters Hall Synod in London it was agreed by a small majority to accept the principle of the sufficiency of the Scriptures rather than manmade tenets as the basis of belief. This gave opportunities for nonconformists to diverge along different paths and was considered by Unitarians as their charter of liberty. Dissenting ministers who could not accept the principle of the Trinity were no longer afraid to declare their views and found support among those Christians who believed in God as one personality, the Son and Holy Spirit being subordinate, Jesus a man approved by God, and the Holy Spirit God's power working through man.

The name 'Unitarian' came to be widely used and accepted

4. Dr Joseph Priestley, aged about 30. From an engraving of the 'Leeds' portrait, c 1764.

after Theophilus Lindsey (1723-1800), a native of Middlewich in Cheshire, resigned his position as Anglican rector to devote himself to literary work on Unitarian beliefs, and published a liturgy to suit Unitarian doctrine. He went to London with fellow Unitarians and took over a room for a temporary chapel in Essex Street in the Strand in 1774 and erected a chapel there in 1778. The Unitarian headquarters today stand on this site, rebuilt after destruction in the Second World War.

Lindsey's friend, Joseph Priestley (1739-1804), was one of the most influential of all Unitarians and closely concerned with Warrington Academy. In his book *The Unitarian Movement in the Religious Life of England* Dr H. McLachlan writes of him as a 'waymaker' both in Biblical and scientific studies, and Alexander Gordon in *Heads of English Unitarian History* comments 'There is scarcely a point on which most independent modern scholars have advanced beyond the outposts of Priestley'. Educated at the Dissenting Academy at Daventry he held Arian and later Socinian views and became a Unitarian minister. Priestley's name is equally honoured among scientists for his discovery of a gas, later identified as oxygen, with all the revolutionary consequences this had for the science of chemistry. While teaching at Warrington Academy he found spare time to work on his scientific experiments which included electricity and optics. He brought to his Biblical studies the same analytical mind, ever searching for the truth and questioning acepted religious beliefs that had no historical basis, or that he considered unreasonable, and was not afraid to express his views. His faith was founded on a belief that both religion and reason proceed from the same God.

When he came to Warrington Academy Priestley found he was among men with the same open-minded views. These were expressed by the Academy's first Principal, Dr John Taylor, in the preface to his *Scheme of Scripture Divinity* which he drew up for the use of his students, in which he adjured them to 'conscientiously attend to evidence as it lies in the Holy Scriptures, or in the nature of things and the dictates of reason' and that they 'assent to no principle or sentiment by me taught or advanced but only so far as it shall appear to you to be supported and justified by proper evidence from Revelation, or reason of things'. Finally he charged them 'to study to live in peace and love with all your fellow Christians; and that you steadily assert for yourselves, and freely allow to others, the unalienable rights of judgement and conscience'.

The 'dictates of reason' also led students at Warrington and other Dissenting academies to adopt a different attitude towards science from the long-held empirical views of the English universities who taught that such evils as disease were a punishment from God. Unitarians did not believe in an avenging God, but looked for the root causes of disease, which lay in poverty and poor housing. Bad drains were the cause of untold unhappiness and they saw it as their Christian duty to get such evils remedied. Followers of Jeremy Bentham (1748-1842), the philosopher, who taught that the highest morality lies in the pursuit of the greatest happiness of the greatest number, were often Unitarians.

This was the whole tenor of teaching at Warrington Academy that closed in 1786, when it was transferred to Manchester and renamed Manchester Academy. Two years before William's

5. The Warrington Academy, artist unknown.

birth it moved again to York and became Manchester New College and was later to play a most important part in his life. The influence of the first Academy continued to be felt in Warrington particularly among members of Sankey Street Chapel, long after its removal. Over four hunded students, lay and divinity, had passed through its doors, the majority being lay students, among them Samuel Gaskell, elder brother of William senior and uncle of William junior, who remained in Warrington until his death in 1848 at the age of eighty-five. Not only would William have come under the influence of Uncle Samuel but he would also have known his grandfather, another Samuel Gaskell, who died in 1813, one of a family of nine children most of whom married and had progeny; so the boy grew up surrounded by numerous uncles, aunts and cousins. The Sankey Street Chapel registers of births, baptisms and deaths are full of Gaskells, many of whom remarried in the Warrington and Liverpool area, residing at Latchford, Warrington, Prospect Hill, Stockton Mount, Woolton Wood and Burtonwood. They were a family of broad interests and tolerant views, many of them prominent in business as well as in chapel affairs and active in services to the local community. Gaskells occur frequently on the lists of committee members of Warrington Library, a subscription library, established in 1760.

As with all Unitarians the Gaskells set a high value on education, considering a study of Latin and Greek essential in the search for truth in the Bible; but scientific studies were not neglected and new engineering methods were of continuing interest to members of the family engaged in industry. To be a member of such a family was to be receptive to both the spiritual and practical aspects of life.

There are no recorded reminiscences of William's childhood and even his exact birthplace at Latchford is not known. It appears that by the time his brother Samuel was born the family had moved to Warrington. The Reverend William Broadbent, minister of Sankey Street Chapel, baptised all six children. They seem to have been a loving and closely knit family, for as they grew up the brothers and sister remained in contact, corresponding, visiting each other and rejoicing in the births of the next generation of Gaskells.

Samuel was born eighteen months after William, then followed three sisters, Anne born in 1808, Margaret in 1810, Elizabeth in 1812, and a third boy Robert in 1814. Margaret died when she was only six and her death must have made a deep impression on the young family, especially on the eleven year old William. In the same year another boy John was born, but tragedy struck the family yet again as William was entering his teens, for his father died in 1819. According to the notice that appeared in the *Monthly Repository of Theology and General Literature* of 1819 above the initials H.G., William senior had been ill for a year and had known of his impending death after rupturing a blood vessel the previous summer. He had faced the inevitable with composure and resignation. H.G. was in all probability his cousin Holbrook Gaskell, as the writer spoke of being with the dying man during the last hours of his life,

6. A view of the Market Place, Warrington, 1840. Lithograph by A. Middleton.

receiving from him instructions regarding the funeral arrangements. H.G. wrote of William's affectionate nature; ever alive to the feelings of want or distress in others. A staunch Unitarian, he devoted much of his time to the study of the Bible and had a wide theological knowledge that he readily passed on to others. He appears to have been a quiet man, happy in his own domestic circle and 'a kind husband and most affectionate father'. He communicated to his eldest son his thirst for knowledge and his keen interest in the Scriptures.

In 1821 the youngest Gaskell child, John, died, so once again young William had to assuage his mother's grief and the responsibilities that he had begun to shoulder since his father's death doubtless gave him a maturity and seriousness beyong his years. His father left considerable assets which, after providing his widow with a hundred pounds a year, were to be used for the education and advancement in life of his young family for which he left detailed instructions to three trustees, all members of the Gaskell family. Having already proved himself an able scholar and a boy who would benefit from a university education it seemed that William was destined for the ministry. Being of an Unitarian family he could not attend an English university, so his name was entered for Glasgow where he was admitted a year after his father's death. This speaks well for the grounding he had received in Latin and Greek and he and his sister Elizabeth are known to have found great pleasure in reading the classics in later life.

William received part of his schooling from the Reverend Joseph Saul, probably acting as private tutor as there is no record of William and his brothers and sisters attending a school. Mr Saul was appointed vicar of Trinity Church, Warrington in 1814. The Gaskells had no reservations about placing their son under the instruction of a minister of the Established Church, for Joseph Saul had a great reputation as a teacher, particularly of the classics. He came from Carlisle where he had been educated at a celebrated local academy run by a relative of his own name and author of a popular arithmetic book. Before taking Holy orders Mr Saul had taught classics at Thorpe Arch Grammar School. He went on to become curate at Newchurch, Winwick, in Cheshire, and proved to be so popular a minister that his congregation subscribed generously for the building of a parsonage for him.

He wrote verses in English, Latin and Greek, and when he came to Warrington he began keeping the parochial records in Latin, noting the number of communicants, the subject of the sermon preached and the total of the collections made. One occasion recorded was when the sermon was chosen to mark the victory at Waterloo and the collection taken was *xii libras, x solidas atque iii denarios*. He enjoyed teaching and readily took pupils for the classics, among them one of the Robson family, who became a well known Warrington doctor and whose brother William married William Gaskell's sister Anne.

Joseph Saul was a fine preacher and continued to enjoy the same popularity as he had attracted at Winwick, but unfortunately this proved to be his downfall. He became so much in demand at social gatherings that he was led into intemperance and when, according to William Beamont in *Warrington Church Notes* of 1878, his wife was involved in 'an act of extreme indiscretion' Joseph Saul was suspended from his duties. But this was in 1821 when William Gaskell's studies had been satisfactorily completed and his tuition under Saul had helped to win him an entrance to Glasgow University. Mr Saul returned to his old academy and became classics master there until his death in 1845. He was never deprived of his living at Trinity Church, where a curate took over his duties until Saul's death. He so far redeemed himself with the Bishop that he was granted permission to hold Divine service at the academy. He continued to write poetry and published a volume of poems in 1831. Mr Saul must surely have sown seeds in his young pupil that later blossomed into young William Gaskell's deep love of the English language and devotion to the classics. The fact that he was ready to enter Glasgow University at the age of fifteen was proof of the excellent schooling he had received.

Shortly after he embarked on his university training his mother married again; her second husband was the Reverend Edward Dimock who became minister at Sankey Street Chapel in 1822 and after the marriage the family moved to Sankey Street. William's studies continued over eight years so he did not spend much time in Warrington nor was much in contact with his stepfather, who appears to have done his duty to his stepchildren for they remained at home with him and their mother until the sons left to embark on careers and the girls married.

Samuel, always spoken of as Sam, was eager to become a doctor, but, being advised against it on account of eye weakness, was apprenticed to a Liverpool bookseller and publisher. During this period he pursued his medical studies on his own and was eventually released by his master and went to Manchester to begin his medical training. In later years when William was living in Manchester Sam was a qualified doctor whom he often consulted on his children's health. Sam was particularly concerned with mental health and was superintendent of Lancaster Asylum from 1840 to 1849 and a member of the Lunacy Commission from 1849 to 1856. Robert too eventually lived and worked in Manchester where he had a thriving business in the leather trade at Patricoft. He married Susan Carpenter, the daughter of a minister at Sankey Street Chapel and he and his wife became frequent visitors to William's home.

Anne was a gentle and delicate girl who grew up to become a loving and warm-hearted woman, and remained in Warrington after marrying the postmaster William Robson to whom she bore two sons. She became a close confidante of William's future wife. Elizabeth, who was always spoken of as Lizzie, was very close to William in his early manhood. She was the one he turned to at the time of his marriage to help him prepare the home for his bride. She seems to have had a keen sense of fun judging by the many touches of humour contained in the letters written to her by William's wife, to whom she became even more closely linked when she married her cousin, Charles Holland. They moved to Liverpool and had nine children. There are glimpses in these letters of a few reservations about Edward Dimock; Mrs Dimock was always referred to by William's wife as 'Mother' but her husband was always Mr Dimock. One letter written to Lizzie in 1833 ends: 'Tell my dear mother how I did enjoy the pears... My blessing (and there are two senses to the words) to Mr Dimock'. The Dimocks moved to Rivington when he was appointed minister of the chapel there in 1841. When Mrs Dimock died in 1850, William's wife wrote that she had died 'full of years surrounded by loving children whom she had brought up to fill their place in the world'.

At no small sacrifice to herself William's mother released him, early in her widowhood, from family ties so that he could set about preparing himself to fill his place in the world.

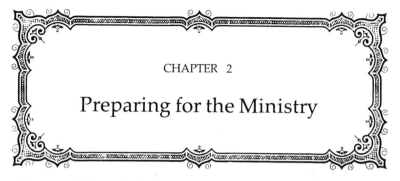

CHAPTER 2

Preparing for the Ministry

Glasgow University had a succession of liberal-minded Professors of Divinity and Moral Philosophy during the eighteenth and
nineteenth centuries and was more willing than Edinburgh to
accept nonconformist students. This made it a natural choice for
William Gaskell's further studies and added to this was the fact
that several Gaskells from the north-west of England had been
educated there in the hundred years before he became a student,
including, most recently, his cousin Thomas Biggin Gaskell, son
of his uncle Roger Gaskell. Thomas matriculated in 1820 but did
not graduate and his death is recorded at the age of twenty-eight
in 1825, so it seems as though his and William's paths never
crossed at Glasgow.

Something of the conditions existing in Glasgow University
during the five years that William Gaskell was a student there
may be learnt from evidence given before the University Commissioner of Scotland in 1827, two years after he had graduated.
It seems that it was not unusual for boys of William's age and
younger to enter the University at that time, and boys from
grammar schools with a good grounding in Latin and Greek had
been admitted as early as ten or eleven years of age; but as the
standards of teaching at grammar schools began to improve boys
were remaining at school longer. At the time William was
accepted as a student no entrance examinations were held and
less value was set on written examinations, which according to
David Murray in his book *Memories of the Old College of Glasgow*
were considered to detract from the University's professed function of 'stimulating thought and promoting culture'. From early
times students were examined orally on the Nones of October

and over the five year course for a Master of Arts degree the student presented himself each year for such an examination before proceeding to the following year's class. William's course of study was as follows: first year Latin, second year Greek, third year logic, fourth year ethics and moral philosophy, by which time he submitted himself for his Bachelor of Arts degree, and then proceeded for a fifth year in natural philosphy, physics, mathematics, astronomy and geography, to obtain his Master's degree.

William's name appears on the college records as having won several prizes, the first the Greek prize for eminence in the Blackstone examination of 1822, and the Mathematics prize for general eminence and a merit award for Ethics in the 1823-4 session. He obtained his Master of Arts degree in 1825 at the age of twenty, having shown himself to be a most able student.

The Blackstone examination took a particular form, common to that adopted at other Scottish universities, and was an important feature of college life. At Glasgow this examination was held in public at the beginning of the University year in the Blackstone Room; students were examined individually by two Professors, one who had been in charge of the student's studies the previous year and the other who would be taking him the following session. The student was examined on two or more books of Greek or Latin prose and poetry of his own choice and was required to read passages aloud, to scan where appropriate, to translate and to answer questions on the text. It lasted twenty to thirty minutes and in William Gaskell's day the timing was measured by means of a sand glass fixed to the back of the **Blackstone Chair on which the student sat facing the examiners;** behind him stood a college official known as the Bedellus, carrying the college mace over his shoulder which he grounded when the sand ran out, uttering the word *Fluxit*. The examiners then declared whether or not candidate had passed. It was considered a disgrace if he failed and set the student back a whole year. Although short it was a thorough and careful examination and one which inspired awe in the candidate, as these verses that were printed in the University periodical of 1817 indicate:

7. The Glasgow University Mace.

8. The Blackstone Chair, Glasgow University showing the sandglass.

For I was born in Glasgow and have sat
Upon that dreaded seat with bottom black;
Ah, seat of terror, to Collegian pale! -
And I have seen the Students gazing round,
And I have sat, and trembling seen the while
Two bushy eyebrows and an under lip,
Were big with meaning. While my every limb
With terror shook, and arch'd each quiv'ring hair.

This was the ordeal that William and his fellow students had to face each year, taking his seat on the famous seventeenth-century chair of dark oak with open arms and elaborately carved back, with a slab of black marble forming the seat. The Black Stone had been in the possession of the University from time immemorial and seems to have a connection with the Scottish belief that an oath taken on a black stone was of a most binding nature. So the Blackstone examination was a solemn occasion and a matter of pride for William when he was awarded the Greek prize, showing him to be the year's best student in the subject considered the most important in the University curriculum.

Today the Blackstone chair is on permanent exhibition in the Hunterian museum of the University, having ceased to be used for the examination after the Universities Act of 1858. The name has been retained in the Cowan (Blackstone) Medal, instituted in 1833, and is still awarded annually for the best student in an oral examination on three set Latin texts.

In William's day students did not live within the college precincts but were either boarded with Professors or had lodgings in the town. Details of students' expenses in 1826 were estimated in the evidence given before the University Commissioner, as between £16 and £17 a year including class fees, books, board, room and rent, on which it was said they were able to live in comfort. Those in humble circumstance could struggle along on a mere 4s a week for food. As classes took up eight hours a day, with four classes of two hours each, William and his contemporaries had little money or time for youthful frivolities. All students were ordered to wear gowns so there were no opportunities for extravagance in that direction. The discipline of these years helped to shape William's character, not moulding him into a dry scholar but into a man ever thirsty for knowledge that he was eager to share with others.

Attendance at Divine service was not compulsory for students not attached to the Church of Scotland. Among his fellow students were Henry Green and Edmund and Sidney Potter. Henry Green became minister of the Unitarian Chapel in Knutsford and remained a lifelong friend. The Potters were Lancastrians and Unitarians and William never lost contact with them though they did not go into the ministry but became by their own endeavours, from humble beginnings, successful in the calico printing trade. They were influential men in the business life of Manchester and were typical of the broad-minded and humane Victorian industrialists who deployed their wealth and energy in public service. Their paths crossed with William's in later life in Manchester and the friendship continued. William spent many holidays with Edmund and his family, who often took a house in Scotland for the summer holidays, where he met, as a child, Beatrix Potter, grand-daughter of Edmund and future author of the *Peter Rabbit* books.

William retained his love for Scotland throughout his life and always enjoyed the bracing air of mountains and was a lover of walking. These formative adolescent years in Glasgow left him with the trace of a Scottish accent and when he became a preacher he was much praised for his clarity of diction which could have been in some measure due to his early association with the clear articulation of the educated Scot.

After graduation William went on to prepare for the ministry at Manchester New College, then at York. Because of the strong influence of those who taught him at York and its close ties with Cross Street Chapel, Manchester, that was to play so vital a part in William's future life it is important to consider in some detail the previous history of this college. It had first been set up in Manchester following the closure of Warrington Academy and partially financed by the proceeds of the sale of that building. It was inaugurated at a meeting in Cross Street Chapel in Manchester in 1786 presided over by Dr Thomas Percival, a leading Manchester physician and former student at Warrington Academy, as were its first two tutors. Dr Thomas Barnes and Ralph Harrison, both ministers at the Chapel. Among later tutors was the eminent man of science, John Dalton, who taught there from 1793 until 1803 and later formulated atomic theory. During that period the classics tutor at the Academy for four years was William Stevenson, father of William Gaskell's future wife. Students at the Manchester Academy, housed in a building in Mosley Street, received a broad education similar to that at Warrington, the majority being destined for commerce but a good proportion were prepared for the law, medicine and the ministry. It was hard to replace men of the calibre of Barnes and Harrison, who had retired by 1800, so it was decided to limit the scope of the Academy to divinity students and this led inevitably to a dwindling in numbers. In 1803 it was determined by the trustees to move the Academy to York, a more central point geographically than Manchester, where a new college would be set up primarily, but not exclusively, for the education of young men for the sacred ministry 'among Protestant Dissenters'. The Manchester property was sold, thus providing a regular source of income for Manchester New College, as it was to be called, and a permanent fund was established that was frequently added to by bequests.

When William became a student at Manchester New College in 1825 he came under the influence of the man who had been divinity tutor at the time of its removal to York and held that position for thirty-seven years. This was Charles Wellbeloved, a name that seems singularly appropriate for a man referred to in later years as 'capable of winning all hearts by his gentleness'. During Wellbeloved's time at the College the title 'Principal' was not used but as divinity tutor he was responsible for its direction so held the position in all but name. It was due to his dedicated teaching that the College attained a reputation for high standards of Christian scholarship that equipped Dissenting ministers with a knowledge in every way equal to that received by members of the Established Church at English universities, and more important, this was imparted in an atmosphere free from dogmatic restraints.

Charles Wellbeloved was born in London and brought up as a Methodist, having as a child sat on Wesley's knee. During his student days at the Dissenting academies of Homerton and then Hackney he became a Unitarian, and took up his first and only ministry at St Saviourgate Chapel, York. After his marriage he began taking private pupils as an additional source of income.

His gifts as a teacher were soon recognised and he built an additional schoolroom to his house to accommodate the increasing number of pupils. It was in this house after his appointment as divinity tutor that Manchester New College had its beginnings until nearby premises were bought in 1811; but Wellbeloved remained in his home and continued to take some pupils as boarders. By this time there were twelve divinity and eleven lay students and two other tutors had been appointed and a visiting examiner, known as a Visitor.

He was a shy, quiet man with deeply held inner convictions of the rightness for him of Unitarianism but with a determination not to indoctrinate his students with his own beliefs but to seek for the truth for themselves. He wrote 'I will not teach Unitarianism nor any other "ism" but "Christianism". I will endeavour to show students how to study the Scriptures and if they find Unitarianism there, well; if Arianism, well; if Trinitarianism, well; only let them find something for themselves; let it not be found for them by their tutor'.

He devoted nearly twenty years of his life to a revised translation of the Bible with a commentary for home use. He worked painstakingly on this huge task but his duties at the College limited the time he could spend on it and he completed only two of the three quarto volumes he had originally planned, the first published in 1828, the second in 1838.

During William's years at York the college buildings comprised a sizeable house that was the residence of one of the tutors, with a lecture hall and classrooms behind, and a row of smaller houses on either side for students' quarters, with a small playing field nearby where pole-leaping and cricket were at the time popular sports; some students went boating on the Ouse. The number of students was between twenty-five and thirty. They had their meals together in the tutor's house in the centre, except for tea which they enjoyed in their own rooms. In their leisure hours they organised debates, glee-singing, Shakespearean readings and brought out a college magazine *The Repository*, shortened to *Poz*.

Certain restrictions were imposed upon the students, a list of regulations being read out at the commencement of their first year of studies, after which they subscribed their signatures and declared their willingness to submit to 'the preceding laws'.

William's signature was appended in September 1825 and the regulations he had heard read were as follows:

i) Every students shall regularly attend such lectures as their tutors shall appoint.

ii) No student shall be absent from the College after evening prayers without leave obtained from one of the tutors, nor after twelve o'clock at night upon any occasion whatever.

iii) No student shall go to any tavern or Inn without leave obtained from one of the tutors.

iv) No student shall go to the theatre or attend the concert oftener than three times without permission of one of the tutors.

v) Dancing in public is altogether prohibited.

vi) At the close of each session an examination of those articles of furniture with which each student has been provided shall take place, when adequate compensation shall be made for any damage which these articles shall have sustained, or shall be replaced by others in good condition at the expense of the student to whose rooms they belong.

vii) A student convicted of the dangerous practice of reading or writing in bed, by candlelight, shall forfeit five shillings.

It was a closely-knit and happy community and during the thirty-eight years that the College was at York the roll of students was only two hundred and thirty-five. Though the primary object of the College was the educating of Dissenting ministers the first three years of the full five year course were planned to meet the needs of lay students. As William already held his Master of Arts degree he was only required to do the final three years at York.

Besides Charles Wellbeloved, William was taught by two former graduates of Glasgow University. One was John Kenrick, a son-in-law of Wellbeloved and like him an outstanding scholar, who was the tutor for classics, history and literature. The other was William Turner, tutor for mathematics, natural and experimental philosophy, logic and metaphysics, who resided at the centre house. This William Turner was the son of William Turner senior, the College Visitor from 1808 until 1859, a former student of Warrington Academy and much loved and long-serving minister at Newcastle-upon-Tyne. His path was to cross William Gaskell's in later years, for it was through

9. John Kenrick. Engraving by Thomas Lupton of a portrait by
George Patten.

Turner senior that William met his future wife, and it was
William who was to preach Turner senior's funeral sermon.

A letter to his father from a fellow student, William Holt of
Liverpool, gave details of the timetable of lectures at that time.
These were usually of a half-hour's duration held from 9.00 a.m.
until 1.00 p.m. and from 5.00 p.m. to 6.00 p.m. on the six
working days of the week. There were prayers in college at 7.45
a.m. and again in the evening, except for students boarding with
John Kenrick, who conducted prayers in his own home. Additional lectures were often held in the afternoon, including Ger-

man given by Mr Kenrick, who also read French privately with this correspondent.

Fellow students of William's with whom he maintained life-long friendships were John Relly Beard, who went on to become minister of Strangeways Chapel, Salford, and worked closely with him in Manchester as a teacher; Edward Tagart, later minister of Marylebone Chapel, London, whom he often visited, and James Martineau, whose first appointment was at Eustace Street, Dublin, then at Paradise Street, Liverpool; later he became Principal of Manchester New College, in Manchester, and then in London from 1869-1885. Dr Martineau, preacher, scholar, and philosopher, by his life and teaching made a great impact on attitudes towards Unitarianism, breaking down resistance to its so-called heresies. He combined the rational approach advocated by Joseph Priestley, with a deeper and more spiritual approach to the Christian life. It must be remembered, however, that while Priestley was a typical man of the eighteenth century, the Age of Reason, and a brilliant scholar and scientist, he was also a man of great piety and a faithful pastor. If he had lived on into the nineteenth century and seen the flowering of the Romantic Movement he would have been able to bring to his teaching a warmer and less polemical approach, embracing the imaginative and mystical aspects of his faith as did Dr Martineau and his contemporaries. It was said of Dr Martineau: 'You have sought to harmonize the laws of the spiritual with those of the natural world and to give each its due place in human life; you have preached a Christianity of the spirit and not of the letter, which is inseparable from morality'.

This was the fraternity of which William was very much a part and there is one sphere of their activities in which he must surely have shared though there is no firm evidence. In 1822 the divinity students had their first chance to go out and preach beyond the College confines. This was in consequence of a petition they had signed asking for permission to go out on Sundays as missionary preachers into the villages within easy reach of York. They realized the importance, for their future roles as ministers, of the ability to speak clearly and often extemporise and to put a clear message across in simple language to the unschooled members of their congregations. Permission was granted and this proved a most successful experiment; students from York

10. Rev William Turner c 1829. Oil painting by Andrew Morton.

were w 'lcomed by ministers of outlying chapels and churches
and in many cases helped to swell the congregations. The elder
William Turner strongly supported this Missionary Society
knowing from his own experience among the poorly educated in
Newcastle-upon-Tyne how essential it was for a preacher to
speak with clarity and simplicity. He advocated the teaching of
elocution at the College and his son presided over a weekly class
on the subject and on occasions these classes were conducted by
an actor from Covent Garden or Drury Lane. The Missionary
Society continued its activities until the College moved from
York and John Relly Beard is known to have been among its most
enthusiastic workers; so it can be fairly assumed that also among
these young missionary preachers was William Gaskell, with
whom he was later to found the Unitarian Home Missionary
Board in Manchester. The influence of the years at York on
William cannot be overestimated. In old age he acknowledged he
debt to the College in these words: 'If I have been of any service
in the world it has been in no large measure owing to the training
received at Manchester College, York'.

He left the College in 1828 to embark on his life's work.

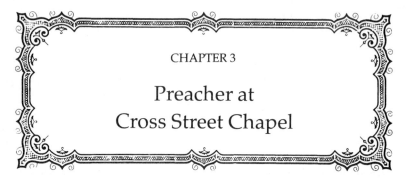

CHAPTER 3

Preacher at Cross Street Chapel

So far, from the known facts of William's early life all that has emerged is a picture of a man carrying on the family tradition of Unitarianism, a dedicated scholar immersing himself in study. Now, as William Gaskell weans himself from his books and puts his scholarship to the service of others, his personality begins to show itself. On 3 August 1828 he was appointed assistant minister to the Reverend John Gooch Robberds of Cross Street Chapel, Manchester. In the sermon that he preached in this chapel fifty years later William referred to 'four spheres of service being open to him when he left college'. There is evidence in the Annals of John Harland, the senior reporter of the *Manchester Guardian* from 1828 and previously reporter on the *Hull Packet*, that William Gaskell was among the candidates for the vacancy at Hull Unitarian Chapel at that period. In the same anniversary sermon that he gave on 4 August 1878, William spoke of his decision to come to Cross Street 'but not without hesitation, for many able ministers had filled the pulpit' and he paid tribute to the sympathy and encouragement he had received from Mr Robberds, who became one of his dearest friends.

So William Gaskell's name was added to the roll of past ministers of the Chapel, men who had entered fully into the religious, social, political and cultural life of Manchester. Cross Street Chapel had been a stronghold of Dissenters in the north-west since it came into existence as a Society without a building in 1682. Its first minister, Henry Newcome, had been attached to the Collegiate Church in Manchester but had been deprived of his Office after refusing to accept the Act of Uniformity that required all clergy to comply with all rites and ceremonies of the

Church of England. He and his many supporters held services in private houses and in a barn, until the chapel building was erected following the passing of the Toleration Act, but this building was burnt down during the Jacobite rising of 1715. Fortunately, Parliament voted a large sum for its restoration. Cross Street Chapel had never been dedicated to any specific form of Christian doctrine but during the ministry of the Reverend Joseph Mottershead (1717-1771) his colleague, Reverend John Seddon, began openly preaching Unitarian, or Socinian, views.

Through its ministers the Chapel had close ties with Warrington Academy and Manchester New College and these connections drew William to this Manchester appointment. In addition his forebears were associated with Cross Street and the early Dissenters, the names Holbrook and Gaskell being the first two entered in the earliest minute book of the Manchester Presbyterian classes, and Nathaniel Gaskell born in 1655 was one of the first trustees of the Chapel and subscribed to the purchase of land for the building.

In other ways William was well fitted for the position. He was a Lancashire man and proud of it and through his family involvement with the manufacture of sail canvas and his friendship with the Potters, owners of the Dinting Vale Calico Printing Works at Glossop, he had an understanding of the problems of the textile trade from the viewpoint of both masters and men. Most important of all was the similarity of the attitudes towards their ministry that were held by William Gaskell and John Robberds. This resulted in a harmonious partnership and a continuity of style in pastoral care that, under these two men, between them spanned over seventy years.

John Gooch Robberds had been at Cross Street since 1811. He was born at Norwich in 1789, and was of Huguenot descent, something shared with James Martineau, with whom he had much in common, particularly a desire to restore to the Unitarian Church the spirituality and warmth that had been lacking since its leaders had become so concerned with reason and rationalisation. In William Gaskell he found a man of like views who, as he had been, was trained at Manchester New College at York under Charles Wellbeloved and John Kenrick. Mr Robberds was married to Mary Turner, the daughter of William Turner, the

11. Greenheys Lane, Manchester, 1827. Sketch by J.W. Ralston.

12. Cross Street Chapel, Manchester, c 1782. Sketch by M. Calver.

Unitarian minister at Newcastle-upon-Tyne who had been the Visitor at Manchester New College during his and William's years as students. John and Mary Robberds lived in the Greenheys district of Manchester, then near to open fields where the workpeople went walking in their free time to escape from the noise and smoke of the mills. They had three children, Charles, Harry and Mary and John Robberds' parents too lived in Manchester. It was a happy and united family and William was soon made to feel one of the circle. He and Mr Robberds shared many interests, particularly a great love of English literature, and evenings of Shakespearean readings regularly held at the Greenheys house were much enjoyed by both men. John had a bright and cheerful nature and was a witty conversationalist, his sense of humour putting William and all his friends immediately at ease. William was keenly interested in the English language and its origins and took a particular delight in punning and play on words. It is unfortunate that very few of his private letters have been kept for it is in personal correspondence that he would have given rein to this facility at juggling with words. Here are two examples from letters that have survived: one to his children in which he signs himself W. Goosequill: the other to his wife written in 1860 apologising for letting out the secret that she was suffering from gout; 'It might show a want of gôut in me to mention it' he wrote. The following year his wife, writing to friends with whom William was going to stay, warns them that 'he is very shy but merry when he is well and he delights in puns and punning'.

It was reserve rather than shyness that was a trait of William Gaskell's character, but it was easily penetrated by family and close acquaintances and by his ever-widening circle of chapel associates who soon became his friends as he entered fully into his busy life as minister. He spoke in later years of those early days when he was welcomed as 'a young untried man'. He soon began to make his mark as a preacher, for in the pulpit he showed no lack of confidence. He went to great pains to prepare his sermons to suit the congregation and the occasion. He once advised a minister who was taking over his Sunday afternoon address to adopt a conversational style, making it like a storytelling with a few lessons included, and to limit it to twenty minutes as parents and children would be sleepy.

William always aimed at making the messages in his sermons simple and clear, couching them in beautiful language, working on them as on a literary composition, taking pains over choice of words and the balance and rhythm of the sentences. In an address he gave to divinity students in 1854 he spoke of language as a great gift that 'God has fearfully and wonderfully made' and of the need to speak out 'in clear strong fitting words the truth of God's solemn message'. He always wrote his sermons out in full, not in note form, but knew them almost by heart so did not need to read them word for word. He regretted that he had not the ability to deliver an extempore address and once said that if he had his time over again he would cultivate this skill 'with the most sedulous care'.

He truly enjoyed delivering his sermons, which he rendered in a fine clear voice, savouring the words. An appreciation of William Gaskell as a preacher was written by John Evans in 1850 in his book *Lancashire Authors and Orators* in which he gave a vivid picture of William's magnetism in the pulpit. But the time John Evans was writing, his popularity as a preacher was established. Every seat was occupied in the chapel on the occasion that Evans went to hear him. He described him standing confidently with his hands resting on either side of the pulpit, a man of prepossessing appearance, slender and of medium height, with a lofty and expansive forehead, with very thick hair ('with a careless parting'), bushy whiskers and bright dark eyes. Every word, spoken in a clear sonorous voice, could be heard; and his message was put across with feeling but no outward gesture. The Reverend J.J. Wright recalling early memories in his book *Young Days* written in 1899, remembers William Gaskell's slender build and the way 'he walked and stood with stately graciousness. There was something clean and sweet and refined and pure in his very presence. It used to be said that his appearance in the pulpit was a sermon in itself as it certainly was a benediction'.

It was not, however, outward appearances that attracted large congregations but the principles of Unitarian doctrine that he was expounding with good sound reasoning. He was soon in great demand as a preacher in outlying chapels, whose numbers gradually increased during William's lifetime. The Victorians demanded elaborate funerals but in the Unitarian church the accent was on the funeral sermon, and very often these were later published as tracts. Many of William's sermons on these solemn occasions have survived in printed form, along with other addresses and lectures in colleges and at ministerial assemblies. He once spoke to students for the ministry, on the secret of success in oratory, saying 'If you would move others you must first be moved yourself'. In the funeral serom that he preached at Cross Street Chapel on 30 April 1854 on the death of his colleague John Gooch Robberds, he was speaking from the heart when he paid tribute to his friend on whose prudence and judgement he had relied for twenty-five years. He spoke of Robberds' piety as being of the bright and cheerful kind so that he would not have wished for the meditation at his funeral to be of a 'gloomy and depressing character'. He referred to Mr Robberds' lively disposition and happy temperament showing itself in his conversation with 'its witty turn and sparkling jests' that could have led those not well acquainted with him into a little misapprehension of his real spirit. 'Religion for him was not something to cover the earth with a cloud but was the light of life touching it with hues of beauty and sending gleams of sunshine into the depths of its darkest shadows'.

Although he was so fine and popular a speaker William Gaskell could never be persuaded to speak on a public platform. He worked for social reforms on numerous committees and held liberal views but never spoke on these issues in public places. Only in the pulpit did he speak out for the dignity of man. From reading his sermons, particularly *The Christianity of Christ* and *The Person of Christ* his firm faith in the good in all men can be discerned. He believed in God as a loving father who did not taint men with original sin, and though weak and fallible all men are capable of goodness and this, he felt, it was his mission as minister to promote. His view of Christ was as a true, real and noble man, divinely appointed but not equal to God, for, he argued, if Christ were God he would be incapable of sin and not tempted at all points as men are. If we regard Christ as a man who can be touched by human frailties we can be inspired by his example.

In the early years of William Gaskell's ministry Unitarians often came under attack from the clergy of the Church of England and were branded as Socinians and heretics. He was never afraid to speak out in defence of his beliefs and on one occasion wrote an open letter to Canon Stowell, the vicar of Christ Church, Salford, who had posed the question 'Is Socinianism Christianity?'. William argued that Unitarians follow Christ's example but pray to the Father only and do not make the Bible bend to creeds. He boldly asked the Canon why he thought he had the right to lay down *his* essentials of salvation, implying that those who did not believe as he did were not Christians. He concluded with the comment that because Unitarians do not agree with Trinitarian creeds this does not mean they are dissenting from Christ. By constant repetition of his beliefs and courteous and reasoned argument, and by the example of his own life William came to be respected by churchmen of all creeds. Proof of this can be found in a letter written in November 1852 by his friend and pupil, Catherine Winkworth, to her sister Emily, neither of them a Unitarian. She wrote 'Mr Gaskell is gaining a great many warm friends in Manchester particularly among the Church clergymen by his activity, good sense and good temper in his committees... He was invited the other day to the distribution of medical prizes which is always done by the Bishop and Dean and to which no Dissenting minister was ever asked before.'

One criticism that was levelled at Unitarianism was that it was only fit for the rich and cultivated, not the gospel of the poor. This was completely refuted by John Robberds and William Gaskell, for although they attracted many of Manchester's intellectuals to Cross Street because of their wide scholarship and cultivated minds, their ability to present a simple message and their friendliness appealed to the working people who first came to know them outside the Chapel.

Much of the work of these two ministers lay among Manchester's poor, whose living conditions were appalling. Housing and sanitation had not kept pace with the growth of Manchester's population after the development of the cotton industry, following the introduction of new machinery in the eighteenth and early nineteenth century. Christianity as practised by the Unitarians meant active concern for your fellow men. Cross Street Chapel provided help through its Domestic Mission, set up between 1832 and 1833 to visit the poor and to help them with the essential needs of life, and to invite them to worship without applying presure. William was secretary of the

Mission for many years. Many of the needs of the children of the working classes were met by the Lower Mosley Street Sunday Schools that originated at Cross Street Chapel, and where William and his wife taught.

Teaching was going to play an increasingly important part in William's life, not only Sunday school children but working men, divinity students and private pupils. He was an inspired teacher. But before these additional duties crowded in upon him William Gaskell had the good fortune to meet the woman who became his partner for life.

This was Elizabeth Stevenson, whom he met at Mr Robberds' house in the auturmn of 1831 where she was visiting with Mrs Robberds' sister Ann. The two young women had recently travelled down to Manchester from Newcastle-upon-Tyne where Elizabeth had just spent two years at the home of the Reverend William Turner, so she and William already had a mutual friend—one who influenced their outlook on life.

Elizabeth was also of a Unitarian background. Her father, William Stevenson, was a one-time minister who had studied and later taught at the Manchester Academy and then became minister at Dob Lane Unitarian Chapel, Failsworth, Manchester. He resigned from the ministry because of certain conscientious

13. Brook Street Unitarian Chapel, Knutsford.

scruples about receiving money as a preacher and became in turn farmer, teacher, writer, editor and finally Keeper of Records at the Treasury in London, where Elizabeth was born. Her mother was Elizabeth Holland, of a Cheshire family of Dissenters who farmed at Sandlebridge near Knutsford. The Stevensons had eight children but only two survived, a son born in 1798 and Elizabeth born in 1810. Mrs Stevenson died when her baby girl was a year old so Elizabeth was taken to Knutsford to be brought up by her mother's sister Mrs Lumb. She had a happy childhood surrounded by loving relations, only occasionally seeing her father who had married again, though her brother John visited her when he was on leave from the Navy. Elizabeth was taught at home until she went to boarding school at Stratford on Avon when she was twelve. She left school just before her seventeenth birthday and spent two years in London, where her father had been taken ill, following the news that John had mysteriously disappeared while on a voyage to India. He was never heard of again. Mr Stevenson died in 1829 leaving little money and Elizabeth, after a short stay with well-to-do Holland relations in London, went up to Newcastle upon Tyne to stay with Mr Turner, to further her education. He was related to the Hollands and had been tutor to some of Elizabeth's cousins.

In Mr Turner's simple household Elizabeth had her introduction to the life of a Unitarian minister and to his involvement with every enterprise for the improvement of social conditions. So when she and William met she had experienced the contrasts between life in the quiet country backwater of Knutsford, in London society and in a northern industrial town. She was beautiful and intelligent, with a natural charm that put all who met her at ease, and had a great sense of fun. She and William found they had much in common, sharing the same religious beliefs, loving literature, music and an unpretentious way of life, and both were fired with a desire to be of service to others. Elizabeth must have been impressed by William's upright stature, his beautiful speaking voice and the enthusiasm that glittered in his dark eyes. His barrier of reserve was soon broken down in her company and their friendship rapidly developed into love. She was now back living in Knutsford and in the spring of 1832 they became engaged and William went down to Knutsford to receive Mrs Lumb's approval.

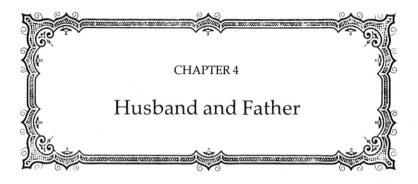

CHAPTER 4

Husband and Father

On 29 August 1832 Elizabeth Stevenson became Mrs Gaskell, a name that was to become famous by the 1850's. His wife's success as a writer was something in which William took a selfless pride. He gave her every support not only with his encouragement and advice but with his ready acceptance of her need to escape 'into the hidden world of art' which, Elizabeth later wrote, 'women needed as a refuge when too much pressed upon by daily small Lilliputian arrows of peddling cares'. No such cares pressed in upon the young couple in the early days of their married life. As their responsibilities increased over the years with the upbringing of a family, William's mounting duties as minister and teacher, and Elizabeth's commitments to literary deadlines, so did their understanding of each other's needs. Their basic unselfishness and mutual love and respect were the foundation on which they made their home a happy, secure and Christian household where they drew their strength to lead full lives. Their home was always open to welcome men and women in all circumstances and they were unsparing in giving of their time to those in need. Elizabeth gave their views in a letter to a friend, written in 1852, on the value of giving time rather than money to others when she referred to 'the number of people who steadily refuse Mr Gaskell's entreaties that they will give their time to anything, but will give him or me tens and hundreds that don't do half the good that individual intercourse and earnest conscientious thought for others would do'.

Their first home was a new house in Dover Street off Oxford Road, Manchester, on the south side of the town and then semi-rural and convenient for Cross Street Chapel and Mr Robberds'

14. Elizabeth Gaskell by G. Richmond, 1851.

house at Greenheys. Before he was married William had lived at No 1 Dover Street with his sister Eliza and the married home was No 14 on the corner of a row of nine newly-built houses and let at a rent of £32 a year. He settled on the house in April soon after his return from their visit to Knutsford to announce the engagement. He had met with Mrs Lumb's whole hearted approval. 'She treated me in the kindest and most affectionate manner and expressed the great pleasure which she felt, that Elizabeth had been led to form an engagement with me', he wrote to Eliza, while Elizabeth writing to her sister-in-law on the same occasion spoke of her aunt's teasing remark 'Why, Elizabeth, how could this man ever take a fancy to such a little giddy thoughtless thing as you?'

By comparison with William's reserve Elizabeth had a natural exuberance and evidence of her happy nature and high spirits can be found in the many letters that she wrote to friends that have survived and are contained in *The Letters of Mrs Gaskell* edited by J.A.V. Chapple and Arthur Pollard and published by the Manchester University Press in 1966. They give a hint of her style of conversation as she rattles on over the page with lively comments on people, places and things. How her bright spirit must have lit up William's home and what strength she must have drawn from the wise and calm masculine presence! In many ways William and Elizabeth were contrasting personalities but each respected the other's viewpoint. By Victorian standards William was the least demanding of husbands, holding views on women's independence that were ahead of his time. Elizabeth once confided to a friend that she was 'sometimes cowardly enough to wish herself back in the darkness where obedience was the only seen duty of women. Only even then I don't believe that William would have commanded me'. She gave an insight into the understanding that existed between them in this passage from her novel *Ruth* where a young wife admits to differing and quarrelling with her husband but 'with a secret joyful understanding with him in her heart, even while they disagreed with each other, for similarity of opinion is not always—I think not often—needed for fullness and perfection of love'.

Their marriage took place at Knutsford Parish Church, not in the old Brook Street Unitarian Chapel attended by Elizabeth and her relatives, as at that time marriages could not be solemnised at Dissenting Chapels.

Elizabeth was married from her aunt's house overlooking Knutsford Heath and her uncle, Peter Holland, a local doctor, gave her away. His daughters were the bridesmaids and William's brother, Sam, the groomsman. Their month-long honeymoon was spent in North Wales, first at the tiny village of Aber near Bangor, and then they travelled by coach to Conway, Caernarvon, Llanberis, Beddgelert and finally to Portmadoc where they stayed with Elizabeth's uncle Samuel Holland, owner of slate quarries at Festiniog. William and Elizabeth wrote a combined letter to sister Eliza while they were in Wales, both brimming over with happiness. William who always loved mountainous scenery spoke of 'the coach ride to Conway, as beautiful as heart could desire. On the left we had Beaumaris and the sea shining and sparkling in the morning light and on our right the hills covered with the warmest tints and the air so fresh and pure and Lily (this was always his name for Elizabeth) looking so very well and two bugles blowing all the way. Wasn't it enough to make one very happy?' Elizabeth wrote in a mocking style of having 'a great deal of trouble with this obstreperous brother of yours. Mountain air seems to agree with us and our appetites admirably'. The same letter contained instructions from William to Eliza to buy a Broadwood piano, place saucers under the plants and to earth up the celery. He could be severely practical at the same time as romantic.

They arrived back in Manchester on 29 September, Elizabeth's twenty-second birthday. For both it was the start of a new phase in their lives, William now had the comfort of a wife to care for his daily needs and to share his responsibilities. For Elizabeth it was a time of greater readjustment. They worked out plans in advance to initiate Elizabeth into her new role. She was writing to their old friend Mr Turner soon after their arrival back to Dover Street telling him that 'Mr Gaskell is going to introduce me to most of the families under his care as their minister's wife and one who intends to try to be their useful friend'. Mrs Robberds had also promised her assistance and advice.

14 Dover Street was their home for the next ten years and during this time William and Lily became 'Papa' and 'Mama'. Their first child was a stillborn daughter born within a year of their marriage, a sad disappointment and their first shared grief; but they were blessed with the safe arrival of another daughter the following year, Marianne, born on 12 September 1834. Two and a half years later Margaret Emily arrived, followed by Florence Elizabeth in 1842, just after they had moved to another house. The young parents were devoted to their little family. William was particularly fond of young children, always ready for a game, but as they grew older his natural reserve made him less demonstrative of his affection than Elizabeth. Her relationship with her daughters was particularly precious, as never having known her own mother, she seemed as though she wanted to compensate her daughters for what she had missed. In Elizabeth's letters there are many references to the orderly but not strict routine of the household and to the simple pleasures

15. Marianne, Meta and Florence Gaskell, 1845. Pastel by Duval.

they enjoyed when the girls were small. Five o'clock was play-time when William danced with the children while she played the piano and 'they make all the noise they can'. Papa took Flossie out flying kites that he had made for her and in the winter he took the children snowballing in the park. On seaside holidays he enjoyed 'pranks and going cockling'. He was as upset as the womenfolk at the death of 'poor dear little Mimi', the family cat.

According to the minutes of Cross Street Chapel committee meeting of 1859 the question of the salary for the second minister was discussed and the sum of £250 was quoted as sufficient remuneration at first, for the services of a younger and inexperienced man. So it can be assumed that in 1832 when William and Elizabeth were newly married this sum, or less, was what he would have been receiving, augmented occasionally by gifts from the congregation. This modest stipend did not allow for many extravagances but both husband and wife had simple tastes and their household was well-ordered and economically run with the help of one maid, Betsy. Visitors to the Gaskells' always found their home comfortable and as one of the Wedgewood family wrote home while staying with them: 'I like all the family arrangements, there is never any bustle and never any dawdling, which makes the beau ideal of domestic occupations and everybody is occupied; the rooms are always tidy and one never sees any tidying'.

The girls had all their lessons at home until they were in their teens and were taught by Papa and Mama and by visiting teachers. William instructed them in history and natural history, Elizabeth taking them for dictation and grammar, as well as such domestic skills as needlework and babycare, for the older sisters, as the babies came along. There was a great deal of reading aloud and this included Bible reading at the daily family prayers. One of their teachers was Rosa Mitchell, who taught them a variety of subjects including Italian. She remained a much-loved friend long after she had finished teaching the girls. French, music, drawing and dancing were among other subjects taught, so, organising a timetable of lessons for girls of different ages, and the coming and going of visiting teachers, called for tactful management. Priority was always given to assuring a quiet retreat where William could withdraw to prepare his sermons, lessons and lectures and deal with his correspondence. He always loved his study and Elizabeth referred to it as his favourite place; he must have been glad to escape to this masculine sanctum away from the stream of callers who began to invade his home as Elizabeth's circle of friends increased and she became more and more involved with charitable work, and here too he could find peace from the girls' piano and singing practice.

Music was always important in the Gaskell household and the eldest girl, Marianne, nicknamed Polly, inherited her parents' love for it. When she was old enough to go away to boarding school, William and Elizabeth chose a school at Hampstead where music was well taught, run by Mrs Lalor, the wife of a Unitarian friend. The second daughter, Margaret Emily, always called Meta, showed an ability at art and went to a school in Liverpool run by Miss Rachel Martineau, and at one period had private lessons from John Ruskin. The Gaskells planned their daughters' education carefully, treating each as an individual and selecting their studies to suit their different aptitudes and abilities. Florence, or Flossie as they called her, was less studious than her older sisters and went to a school at Knutsford run by the Unitarian minister, Henry Green, who had been William's fellow student at Glasgow University. He and his wife were intimate friends of Elizabeth, whom she frequently visited when staying with her Knutsford relations. Henry Green christened Marianne at Knutsford and the little Gaskell daughters sometimes stayed with the Greens.

Apart from helping to supervise their lessons, William appears to have entrusted the upbringing of the girls mainly to Elizabeth. Never a dominating father, he was dearly loved and much respected by his daughters. There are many cautionary remarks in Elizabeth's letters to her girls when they were away at school, warning them against actions that may displease Papa. When Marianne was invited to stay with people whom William feared would not be a good influence, Elizabeth wrote advising her not to stay for more than two days. 'Papa, I know, would not like it'. Elizabeth complained confidentially to a close friend that it was not easy to talk to William about anxieties, but it is more than likely that he was keeping his own feelings in check and adopting a detached attitude to counteract Elizabeth's over-anxiety about her children. There is no doubt, however, that in times of trouble he was the rock on which she leaned. When Marianne was four years old and badly affected by croup William sent for his brother Sam, then a doctor in Manchester, and the two men sat up all night with the child. When Flossie was eleven years old and rather delicate it was William who saw to it that she had half a glass of port each morning. It was Sam who recommended the sea air of Morecambe Bay when Marianne was frail as a baby. This became one of the family's favourite haunts, especially Silverdale. Elizabeth's health suffered from the effect of Manchester's smoky atmosphere and William insisted on her frequently taking short breaks away from home at the seaside or in the country and she would return refreshed. He was not always able to join her because of his chapel duties but when he did so their enjoyment was intense. Here is a description of a few days they had away together in 1838 with a chapel friend at Rivington Pike. 'Oh, Rivington is such a pretty place and so thoroughly country' she wrote. 'Yesterday morning I sketched... and in the evening we both rode on horseback up and down the country then a walk after tea. This Rivington air has done wonders and made me so strong and happy and hungry. Good air for ever!'

Never was William's calm presence more needed than in 1844 when the Gaskells suffered a shattering blow in the loss of a baby boy at eleven months old. He was born two years after Flossie in the house at 121 Upper Rumford Street, where they had moved from Dover Street in 1842. It was only one street away but it overlooked fields. They needed a larger house for the growing family and, as their financial position had improved in recent years, this was now possible. Manchester New College had moved from York to Manchester in 1840 and William's appointment there as secretary and later lecturer increased his earnings. In addition, Elizabeth had inherited a legacy of £80 a year, on the death of Mrs Lumb in 1837. They were able to afford more domestic help; Miss Fergusson who stayed for a few years as nanny, and Miss Hearn who remained a faithful servant and trusted friend of the family for twenty-five years. So now with the crowning joy of the birth of a son and heir, the pleasure of the new home, the satisfaction of his additional duties at the College, William was feeling confidently happy, and rejoicing at

Lily's delight in Baby William. He was a contented and healthy baby and his sisters were each given little tasks to help Mama in caring for him. In the summer of 1845 when little William was nine months old the Gaskells went to Wales for some seaside air. Marianne caught scarlet fever while they were there and made a good recovery but her little brother sickened and died from the illness at Portmadoc on 10 August. He was buried in the churchyard of William's old family chapel in Sankey Street, Warrington, and the family returned home to the house that for Elizabeth thereafter would be filled with memories of their little son's brief life. William must have recalled the days of his boyhood when he had watched his parents facing the deaths of his sister Margaret and brother John. He knew that he and Lily had to face and overcome their grief and sublimated his own sorrow in an effort to lift his wife from the depths of depression that engulfed her, even when she found she was expecting another baby. He found the solution to the problem by encouraging Lily to try her hand at writing a novel. With his support she set about the task and continued with it after the arrival of their fourth daughter, Julia, on 3 September 1846. The new baby rapidly became 'the pet of the house' and as she grew up developed a lively and endearing personality.

Elizabeth completed her novel *Mary Barton* by the end of the following year and achieved an unforeseen success with it, which in many ways brought about a change in the pattern of the Gaskell family life, but strengthened rather that jeopardised the ideal partnership of William and Lily.

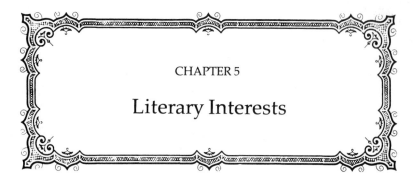

CHAPTER 5

Literary Interests

William's suggestion that Elizabeth should attempt a full length book was a serious one, not a desperate remedy for her depression aimed solely at occupying her mind. He knew of her ability as a writer, not only as a fluent letter writer but as a writer of short stories for her own amusement and for her Sunday School classes. Words flowed easily from her pen as was evident in the long and vivid letters she wrote to friends and relations, many of which she let William read as is known from her comments in a letter to Lizzie Gaskell in 1838. 'When I had finished my last letter Willm. looked at it and said it was "slip-shod" —and seemed to wish me not to send it... the sort of consciousness that Willm. may at times and generally does see my letters makes me not write so naturally and heartily as I think I should do... Still I chuckled when I got your letter today for I thought I can answer it with so much more comfort to myself when Wm. is away which you know he is at Buxton'.

His reading of her letters should not be seen as an instance of William's desire to dictate to her over their contents but as an indication of the trust that existed between them, so that Elizabeth would, as a matter of course, pass over any letter to Lizzie asking him if he had anything to add, as he did in a footnote to a letter of December 1838 when he wrote: 'Dear Lizzie, I've only just time to send my love to you and Charles and Anne which Lily in her hurry has forgotten'. It was because so many of her letters were such spontaneous outpourings of her high spirits written in a conversational manner that they contained errors in spelling, grammar and punctuation that would not be up to William's precise standards. In a later letter to her publisher she

apologises for using two sentences 'with "so" in them not followed by "as" as Mr Gaskell says they ought to be' and concludes
with one grammatical sentence as an example: 'I am *so* much
obliged to you *as* to be incapable of expressing my obligation'.
Even when his elder daughters were in their twenties and Flossie
eighteen and writing home to him while on holiday with their
mother in Germany, he wrote to Elizabeth: 'Thank the children
all for their notes and good wishes—(but *between* you and me
their spelling is a trifle too phonetic, and we must try to reform
it)'.

In their early married life it was William's and Elizabeth's
shared love of poetry that set their minds working on the value of
unsophisticated verses, to inspire the simple minds of the
uneducated masses. In the same way as a child is attracted by the
lilt and word patterns of nursery rhymes and hymns so, they felt,
could the unschooled working man and woman learn to love the
sound of words and master their meaning. They could absorb a
message put across in lines of verse that they could commit to
memory, far more easily than through any amount of admoni-
tory passages of prose. They were impressed by the numbers of
Lancashire working men who had a natural ability at using to full
effect the rich and varied Lancashire dialect words. Such men as
Samuel Laycock, Edwin Waugh, Ben Brierley, John Critchley
Prince and Samuel Bamford were writing verses at that period
that expressed with unsentimental poignancy the plight of the
poor, and struck a chord with their fellow workers because they
told in everyday speech of experiences common to all. Samuel
Bamford was personally known to them both and Mrs Gaskell
chose to quote from his verses ' God Help the Poor ' in *Mary
Barton*, referring to them in the story as 'Bamford's beautiful little
poem'. This is one of the verses from it.

> God Help the poor! Behold yon famished lad,
> No shoes, nor hose, his wounded feet protect;
> With limping gait and looks so dreamy sad,
> He wanders onward, stopping to inspect
> Each window stored with particles of food.
> He yearns but to enjoy one cheering meal;
> Oh! to the hungry palate viands rude,
> Would yield a zest the famished only feel!

He now devours a crust of mouldy bread;
With teeth and hands the precious boon is torn;
Unmindful of the storm that round his head
Impetuous sweeps. God help thee, child forlorn!
God help the poor!

William realized that through poetry lay one way in which he could communicate with the people he was so eager to help. He began to prepare a course of lectures for working men on the subject 'Poets and Poetry in Humble Life' and enlisted Elizabeth's help in reading and selecting from the work of suitable poets. In a letter of 1836 Elizabeth tells her sister-in-law of the delight she was finding in 'doing Coleridge and Wordsworth, having already 'done' Crabbe and being 'anxious to get on with my poets'. Their interest in the poetry of Crabbe, who wrote 'Scenes from Humble Life' in the late eighteenth century, describing the hard lives of the fisher folk and countrymen in his native county of Suffolk, prompted William and Elizabeth to attempt some similar verses about Manchester's poor. Using the same metre as Crabbe and rhyming couplets they started on *Sketches Among the Poor* and sent the first to *Blackwood's Edinburgh Magazine* that was published in the January issue of 1837, merely titled No. 1, and their names did not appear. The subject of this poem was Mary, a humble working woman living alone in a dark house in a gloomy street but who was never sad or lonely because she lived a life of service to others and was always remembering her childhood days in the country where she hoped one day to return. It contained these lines:

It was a pleasant place that early home!
The brook went singing by, leaving its foam
Among the flags and blue forget-me-not;
And in a nook, above that shelter'd spot,
For ages stood a gnarled hawthorn tree,
And if you pass'd in spring-time you might see
The knotted trunk all coronal'd with flowers,
That every breeze shook down in fragrant showers;
The earnest bees in adorous cells did lie
Hymning their thanks with murmuring melody.

This was the only one of the *Sketches* that they wrote, for Meta was born in the February of the same year, and Elizabeth never attempted to write any other poetry for publication. It seems as though the character described in this first *Sketch* could have been based on someone known to William and Elizabeth who had impressed them by her gentle and unselfish nature and quiet acceptance of her humble lot. In *Mary Barton* the character of old Alice Wilson bears a close similarity to the Mary of the poem. She too speaks longingly of her country home where as a girl she would 'sit down under the old hawthorn tree where we used to make our home among the great roots as stood above the ground'.

William's interest in bringing poetry to the people and encouraging local poets never waned and the course of lectures that he prepared proved extremely popular. He tried them out at home on his family and friends. On one occasion Elizabeth lay on the sofa and enjoyed herself listening with Sam Gaskell and Mrs Robberds and they were as impressed by William as his audience had been when he lectured on Burns at Miles Platting, one of the poorest districts in Manchester and 'was famously clapped'. He went on to prepare a second series and again Elizabeth wrote of 'picking up with all the Poets in Humble Life we can think of'.

16. Hints on English Composition', lecture notes by William Gaskell on the importance of harmony and literary taste. Manuscript discovered behind a bookcase in his study.

At the same time William was turning his own poetic talents to hymn writing, both original hymns and translations from the German. His friend John Relly Beard, a former fellow student at New College and now Unitarian minister at Strangeways Chapel, Salford, brought out a collection of five hundred new hymns in 1837 to which William contributed over seventy. They were written by invitation rather than inspiration and were in conventional form, easy to find a tune to and condusive to the atmosphere of worship. Each hymn carried a lucid and pious message to inspire the simple and homely people whose hearts he sought to touch. They are described by the Rev. Raymond Cook, the present minister at Cross Street Chapel, as hymns which can be likened to a 'soft flute' not a 'brazen trumpet'. Here are two, which are contained in *Hymns of Worship* and are still sung today.

No. 508

O God! the darkness roll away
Which clouds the human soul
And let Thy bright and holy day
Speed onward to its goal!

Let every hateful passion die
Which makes of brethren foes,
And war no longer raise its cry
To mar the world's repose.

How long shall glory still be found
In scenes of cruel strife,
Where misery walks, a giant crowned,
Crushing the flowers of life?

O hush, great God, the sounds of war,
And make Thy children feel
That he, with Thee, is nobler far
Who toils for human weal.

Let faith, and hope, and charity,
Go forth through all the earth;
And man in holy friendship be
True to his heavenly birth.

No. 372

Though lowly here our lot may be,
High work we have to do,
In faith and trust to follow him
Whose lot was lowly too.

Our days of darkness we may bear,
Strong in a Father's love,
Leaning on his almighty arm,
And fixed our hopes above.

Our lives enriched with gentle thoughts
And loving deeds may be -
A stream that still the nobler grows,
The nearer to the sea.

To duty firm, to conscience true,
However tried and pressed,
In God's clear sight high work we do,
If we but do our best.

Thus may we make the lowliest lot
With rays of glory bright;
Thus may we turn a crown of thorns
Into a crown of light.

William's own copy of Dr Beard's *Collection of Hymns for Private and Public Worship* is now in the possession of Manchester College, Oxford. It contains, in his own handwriting, on the back pages an additional hymn. This is entitled 'Hymns for the Cottage':

Child of labour! lift thine head,
    Think not meanly of thy state;
Let thy soul be nobly fed,
    Thine shall be a noble fate.

See, for thee this wondrous earth,
  Made and beautified by God;
Thine as his of proudest birth
  Who its pathways ever trod.

Meekly take thy part assigned,
  Let its evils be withstood,
And thy soul ere long shall find
  Holy use turns all to good.

Ne'er forget thy being's end,
  Ne'er let go thy spirit's faith,
Hope and thought for comfort send
  Onward past the reach of death.

Feel a Father ever nigh,
  Calmly rest upon his love:
Soon his hand thy tears shall dry,
  In the realms of light above.

Have these simple and appealing verses ever been sung?
William's copy also contains a number of amendments to his
hymns, sometimes verses completely rewritten or lines
rephrased or rhymes improved. This suggests that he may have
been pressed to meet a deadline for the printing of the book so
was unable to give the verses the necessary polishing that he
would have wished. In leisure hours he later made such
improvements as these examples show. (William's alterations
are in brackets).

Hymn 228 (verses 2, 3 and 4)
After a death in congregation

Who next shall leave a vacant place,
  Where he was wont to dwell, (And thro' the death shade go)
Whose next shall be the missing face,
  Thou, God, (Lord) alone canst tell! (dost know!)

Or young, or old, not one can say
    'That lot shall not be mine;
Not one declare (presume) another day
    Upon his path will shine.

Then may we all to wisdom give
    The moments as they fly,
That we may be more meet to live,
    And yet prepared to die.

(And teach us so with Thee to live,
    And fix our thoughts on high,
That when the summons Thou shall give
    We may not fear to die.)

Two years later William brought out a book of temperance rhymes. Going about his pastoral duties he was often brought face to face with drunkenness and its effect of family life. William had a humanitarian attitude to the problem of drink and in his understanding of the drunkard's craving comes close to the modern acceptance of alcoholism as a disease and the sufferer as an object of pity not of condemnation. He expressed his feelings in the dedication that he made in his *Temperance Rhymes:* 'To The Working Men of Manchester. These rhymes are inscribed in the hope that they may act as another small weight on the right end of that lever which is to raise them in the scale of humanity'. In his poem 'The Slave' he expressed vividly the agony of a man who had made himself a slave to drink. It includes these verses:

Ah! once I was a freeman true
    And boldly looked around,
Now if my eyes meet those I know
    They straight are on the ground.

Once not a touch of fear I felt
    Go whereso'er I might'
Now strangling terrors like a belt
    Gird me both day and night.

The same anguish is expressed in the following:

Song

Oh! the hours that I have lost,
　　Lingering o'er the maddening bowl;
Bartering health and strength for pain,
　　Darkening still life's darkened scroll;
Ah! those hours so vilely slain
Would I had them back again!

Oh! the powers that I have lost,
　　Dimmed and deadened and defaced;
Leaving on my soul a stain,
　　Time can never see erased;
Ah! those powers, so lent in vain,
Would I had them back again!

Oh! the friends that I have lost,
　　Wounded, grieved and spurned away;
Laughing when they did complain,
　　Mocking when they turned to pray;
Ah! those friends so pierced with pain,
Would I had them back again!

While William was writing hymns and rhymes Elizabeth had turned her hand to prose and in 1838 had her first literary success with an article on Clopton Hall, Warwickshire, printed in a series on *Visits to Remarkable Places* published by William and Mary Howitt, who edited a journal. Her name did not appear nor did she receive payment but the contact with the Howitts was to prove fruitful. A friendship developed through correspondence and in 1841 William and Elizabeth met the Howitts for the first time during a holiday in Germany where they stayed during William's annual month's leave. This was one of the few holidays that Elizabeth and William enjoyed together abroad. At that time they had only two daughters who were cared for by Knutsford relations but as their family increased they were reluctant, particularly William, to leave the children in the hands of others, so took their holidays in England.

17. William Gaskell c 1869, from the Cross Street Chapel
photograph album.

They enjoyed their sightseeing in Germany, especially visiting the cathedrals. Elizabeth referred in a letter to 'the practical poetry of the architecture' and went on to describe having tea with the Howitts who were living in Heidelberg for a while, in considerable style. 'My word,' she commented, 'authorship brings them in a pretty penny'. Little did she know that authorship was going to earn her sufficient money to enable them all to take further holidays abroad. After the birth of Florence and little William they settled on holidays nearer home at Silverdale on Morecambe Bay and frequent visits to North Wales which was where they suffered the loss of their little boy.

Elizabeth started on her novel in 1845 and spent two years on it choosing a subject that both she and William felt very deeply about, the sharp contrast between the lives of the rich and poor in Manchester in the eighteen-forties. William gave her every support, furnishing her with facts and figures so that the picture she gave of the living conditions of the weavers and their families, round whom she built her story, were undeniably true. Through William she had access to the reports made to the Cross Street Domestic Mission by John Layhe, Minister to the Poor. The central drama of the book was built round the murder of a millowner by the weaver John Barton, father of Mary, and this was an echo of a real event that took place in the eighteen-thirties when a Thomas Ashton of Werneth, near Hyde, was murdered after a dispute with the trades union, but not directly based on it. William's hand is seen in the able rendering of the Lancashire dialect as he had made a close study of this and lectured on the subject. Being a native of the county he had an ear for the sound and rhythm of the everyday speech of Lancashire folk that Elizabeth would have found hard to capture, let alone to spell!

When the book was well advanced she sent the manuscript to the Howitts, who offered to act as her agents with the publishers Chapman and Hall, who agreed to publish it. William went to London with her to see the publishers and a payment of £100 was agreed for the copyright and the book was to appear under the pseudonym Cotton Mather Mills Esq., a name Elizabeth had already used for three stories that she had supplied the Howitts with for their journal in 1847.

When *Mary Barton* was published in 1848 it contained explanatory notes by William on the dialect and he also wrote some of the short lyrical headings that accompanied every chapter. He was the writer of those that were ascribed 'Manchester Songs'. None expresses more aptly the message of *Mary Barton* than these lines of William's that preface Chapter VI 'Poverty and Death':

> How little can a rich man know
> Of what the poor man feels,
> When Want, like some dark demon foe,
> Nearer and nearer steals.
>
> *He* never tramp'd the weary round,
> A stroke of work to gain,
> And sicken'd at the dreaded sound
> Which tells he seeks in vain.
>
> Foot-sore, heart-sore, *he* never came
> Back through the winter's wind
> To a dank cellar, there no flame,
> No light, no food to find.
>
> *He* never saw his darlings lie
> Shivering, the flags their bed;
> *He* never heard that maddening cry,
> Daddy, a bit of bread!

Later editions contained the text of the two lectures on dialect that William delivered in Manchester in 1854. He had a firm belief that the Lancashire dialect is not a corruption of modern English but contains traces of the language of the early Britons and has much in common with Welsh. His theory was that the Anglo-Saxons did not conquer the north-west until some two hundred years after their invasion of Britain and natives who had fled there still used the old tongue. He concluded his lectures with an apology for being unable to squeeze into two hours all that he could wish and finished with the apt quotation 'A man canno' do more nor he can, how can he?'

He was always modest about his literary work and it was Elizabeth's promptings that brought about the inclusion of these lectures in *Mary Barton* in the 1854 edition. William's attitude seems to have been that the publisher was doing him a favour by printing them. 'He did not like Mr Chapman to be put to any expense on his account', wrote Elizabeth. After the publication of *Mary Barton* the true identity of Cotton Mather Mills was soon revealed and Elizabeth was hailed as a writer of promise, particularly by Charles Dickens, who sought her work. Other books and stories followed in steady succession, *Cranford* and *North and South* appearing in serial form in Dickens' magazine *Household Words*.

William read through and checked all Elizabeth's work for grammatical, spelling and factual errors before it went to the publisher and also helped her with the proof reading. They clearly discussed together the terms and payment for each publication, and he dealt with the banking of the money as at that time married women could not open a bank account. He appears to have put no restrictions on how she spent the money for she was careful and provident and taught their daughters to care for their clothes and not to indulge in extravagant tastes. The money she earned was spent liberally, however, on holidays abroad and extra tuition for the girls. As her earnings increased when the books ran to several editions and the short stories were being reprinted as collections, and much of her work was being sold abroad, William helped with the business side of her career. He preferred her to receive royalties and was against outright payment to which she inclined in the early days.

No book involved them both in more difficulties than *The Life of Charlotte Brontë* published after Charlotte's death. The two women novelists had met in 1850 and a friendship rapidly developed. Subsequently Charlotte visited Plymouth Grove and met William for the first time. She described him in a letter as 'Mrs Gaskell's long, lean and scholarly husband' and pronounced him 'a good and kind man'. When she married the Reverend Arthur Nicholls, who was prejudiced against Unitarians, Charlotte confided to a friend that 'if he could come to know Mr Gaskell it would change his feelings'. It took Elizabeth two years to write the biography, and William's help was readily given in checking and advising on this piece of work that required scrupulous editing, as so many living people were concerned. Elizabeth went abroad for a holiday with two of the girls to Rome a few days before its publication in order to avoid the publicity she always shunned.

It fell to William to handle the delicate situation that arose on the publication of the book. A court case was threatened over references to the part played in the downfall of Branwell Brontë by Mrs Robinson, his one-time employer. William had to take quick action without consultation with Elizabeth and speedily put the matter in the hands of their solicitor friend, William Shaen, who drew up a retraction and an apology that was printed in *The Times*. All unsold copies were withdrawn, the book having already gone into a second edition. After Elizabeth's return an expurgated text was prepared for the third edition.

The years that Elizabeth was involved with the writing of the biography coincided with the period of a rapid increase in William's duties. Mr Robberds had died in 1854 so he was now the senior minister at Cross Street, with James Ham appointed as his assistant in 1855. Since 1840 he had been secretary of Manchester New College when it returned to Manchester from York and six years later he was appointed as Professor of English History and Literature to the College. In 1854 he played a prominent part in the founding of the Home Missionary Board in Manchester where he became tutor of English literature and later Principal. By now it was obvious to William that there was little time for him to devote to his own literary efforts apart from the many hours he spent preparing his sermons, lectures and lessons. His role was to infect others with a love of English literature and leave creative writing to his wife. One of his pupils and close friend, Catherine Winkworth, wrote of how much she had gained under his guidance and had been stimulated by 'his rich and varied culture, rare critical power and exquisite refinement of taste. We have often regretted that his unselfish and lifelong devotion to religious and benevolent labours for others should have left him so little time and opportunity for original work of his own especially in history and criticism'.

A literary outlet of a different nature presented itself in 1861 when William became joint editor with John Relly Beard, Brooke Herford and John Wright, of the *Unitarian Herald*, a weekly newspaper costing a penny. It was founded by Manchester Unitarians who felt the need for an additional organ to interest a wider public in Unitarian attitudes than the already existing newspaper the *Inquirer*. From 1865 William and Brooke Herford were in sole charge and it was a successful and widely read paper

18. Headquarters of the Manchester Lit. and Phil., George Street, Manchester.

until a third journal the *Christian Life* came out in 1876, when its circulation declined. All three papers were eventually amalgamated, but not in William's life time. He carried out his editorial duties conscientiously, putting in six or seven hours a week at the Manchester office as well as 'a great deal of odd time at home' as Elizabeth complained to her sister-in-law in 1865, wishing that he would withdraw from this duty but added 'he meets with people he likes; and all the subjects he is engaged upon interest him very much'.

William was able to meet with kindred spirits unconnected

with his ministerial duties through membership of the Manchester Literary and Philosophical Society and the Portico Library. Members of Cross Street Chapel were closely concerned with both these bodies from their beginnings. Dr Thomas Barnes, the only minister of religion amongst the earliest members of the Literary and Philosophical Society, was one of the first secretaries on its foundation in 1781 and for nearly twenty years the society's meetings were held in the chapel room at Cross Street. By the time William became a member the society had premises in George Street. He was a member for thirty-eight years and became one of the vice-presidents in 1871.

Among the chief promoters of the Portico Library in Mosley Street, founded in 1806, was Samuel Kay, a secretary of the Cross Street Chapel trustees for over forty years. The stated objects of the Library were 'to gratify the thirst for knowledge and promote a greater degree of intercourse among the town's inhabitants', aims with which William Gaskell was in complete sympathy. In course of time he took on the responsibility of Chairman of the Library and held this position from 1849 until his death. Being so keen a student and booklover, to whom the library bookshelves must have been an allurement, William Gaskell found little time for private study for his own gratification. While Elizabeth was winning the hearts of the reading public with her writing, William was illuminating the minds of students of every age and class with his teaching.

19. Mosley Street, Manchester, 1824. The Portico Library is one the left and St Peter's Church (now demolished) at the end. Engraving by John Fothergill.

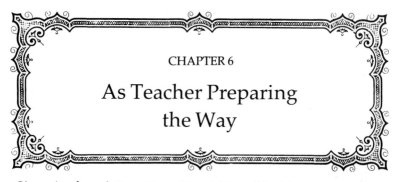

CHAPTER 6

As Teacher Preparing the Way

Since its foundation Cross Street Chapel had been generating interest in learning at all levels, in literature and science as well as in Biblical studies, as had been early made manifest by the setting up of the Manchester Academy and the Manchester Literary and Philosophical Society; both institutions held their early meetings in Cross Street Chapel Room in the seventeen-eighties. When William Gaskell became junior minister the chapel was attracting to its services men and women of culture, many of them not committed Unitarians, but who found stimulation in fellowship with others of inquiring minds. Many of its congregation were members of the colony of German textile merchants who had settled in Manchester and found at Cross Street the form of worship closest to that of their homeland, and they infused fresh blood into the society. However, Cross Street Chapel was by no means an enclosed enclave of intellectuals but a fraternity who saw it as their Christian duty to give their time, talents and money to public service.

Christ's commandment 'Feed my lambs' was interpreted by Unitarians as an injunction that embraced the broader implications in the tenet 'Man cannot live by bread alone'. Philanthropy in Victorian times changed its guise from the Lady Bountiful of earlier days, with basket on her arm distributing loaves and clothing to the poor, to one of Sunday School teacher bringing warmth and light into classrooms, for the overworked and poorly nourished children of the working classes. This was the era of self-help as propounded by Samuel Smiles in his book of that name, author also of the 'Lives of the Engineers' when such self-educated men as James Brindley and George Stephenson were glorified.

Education was the starting point for self-help and as early as 1734 Cross Street Chapel had started a charity school to teach reading, writing and arithmetic to the children of Dissenting Protestants: 'not excluding others' being added with true Unitarian tolerance. This was a day school with separate departments for boys and girls and an addition was built on to the back of the Chapel to accommodate 40 scholars. By the time William came to Manchester this school had been transferred to Mosley Street, started when Manchester's second Unitarian Chapel was built there in 1789. Teachers at these schools were appointed by the Chapel and they received much voluntary help from chapel members. A full account of these schools and their successors has been given by Lester Burney in *Cross Street Chapel Schools* published in 1977, so it is sufficient to take up the story when plans were afoot for the schools' next removal in 1832, the year of William's marriage. He and John Robberds were on the committee appointed in that year to superintend the establishment of new schools on a different site.

Mosley Street Chapel and adjoining premises had been bought by a business man for commercial development and a new chapel was to be built in Brook Street. A site was found for the new schools at the corner of Lower Mosley Street and Windmill Street and the building was completed four years later, the schools being renamed the Lower Mosley Street Schools. Both William and Elizabeth had experience of teaching at the earlier premises which were cramped and inadequate, the boys meeting in a cellar under the Mosley Street Chapel and the girls in premises across the yard behind the Chapel and in a room above the organ loft. They continued to take an active part in the new schools, William both in an administrative capacity as a committee member and as minister, taking the Sunday evening service held in the school after classes in turn with John Robberds and John Tayler, minister of Brook Street Chapel; Elizabeth taught at the girls' Sunday school and became involved with visiting the homes of her pupils and in this way gained that insight into the lives of Manchester's poor that she depicted with such power in *Mary Barton*. The Sunday School girls visited Plymouth Grove once a month when this became the Gaskells' home.

The first headmaster appointed to the Lower Mosley Street

Schools was John Curtis and under his dedicated leadership the number of scholars steadily increased. In 1837 there were 407 scholars, and according to Catherine Winkworth, a friend of the Gaskells who taught at the school with her sister, Susanna, the numbers had reached 1500 by 1848. The Winkworth sisters were among many men and women who volunteered their help as teachers in this great Christian task of bringing light into the dark pits of ignorance into which so many seemed destined to pass their lives. Their work did not stop in the classroom for it was common practice for Sunday school teachers to visit the homes of all those who had been absent on the previous day, not in a spirit of inquiry but of concern for their welfare. This was done without condescension or patronage and helped to break down the rigid class barriers of the times.

20. The corner of King Street and Cross Street, Manchester, c 1820.

Other barriers had to be broken that had been erected by certain elements of the Protestant Church who criticised the teaching of subjects other than religious knowledge on Sunday. They seemed unaware of the fact that in a city like Manchester many of the young people were at work all the week in mills and factories and Sunday was the only day when there was time to teach them basic skills to equip them for adult life. William Gaskell countered this criticism most ably in an address he gave to the Manchester and District Sunday School Association in Bolton in 1850. He said that the teaching of the alphabet should be considered by the teachers as service in the Temple where

21. 1851 Ordnance Survey map showing the ground floor layout of the Lower Mosley Street Schools and the surrounding area densely packed with mills and dwelling houses.

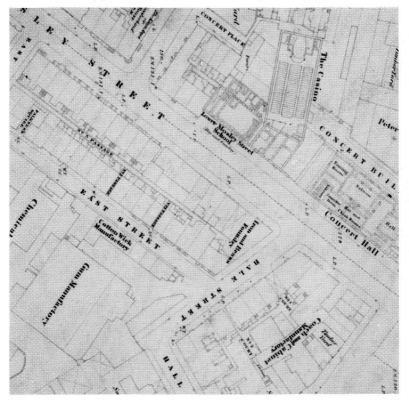

they were 'about their Father's business'. In the same address he stressed the importance of the dual role of the Sunday School teacher, both inside and outside school. He appealed to them to bring to teaching 'a loving heart' and to prepare their minds for their work by 'gathering in knowledge' so as to make their lessons attractive. He explained how, by visiting their pupils' homes, they could dispel parents' fears that they were trying to draw the children away from the family. They should strive to be accepted as friends of children and parents alike, and by helping with material comforts would be able to progress to spiritual comforts. He ended with the words: 'Let it be seen that you do all to the Glory of God. You will be silently and constantly instilling into their souls the genuine piety which, brought into a family,

22. The Lower Mosley Street Schools, from a watercolour. The roof of the Central railway station can be seen on the left.

draws after it all other good'. Seven years later William preached the funeral sermon on the occasion of the death of John Curtis and paid high tribute to this man who had been headmaster of Mosley Street Schools for twenty-two years. 'The work that our friend had to do', he said, 'is one of the highest and holiest to which a human being can consecrate his efforts'.

Under John Curtis' headmastership many pupils had risen from the ranks to become teachers and from among them emerged his successor, George Smith. William Gaskell was particularly interested in the teaching of young adults and his own energies were channelled in this direction after 1840, when much of his time was claimed by his old academy Manchester New College, that returned from York to Manchester in that year. The

23. The Jubilee Medallion, struck to commemorate the fiftieth anniversary of the Lower Mosley Street Schools in 1886.

move back came after London University had been founded and there was a feeling at York that the College should consider a removal to London to serve as a training college for divinity students. Others favoured a return to Manchester as the population was steadly increasing and there were many active nonconformists in the area with whom students would be in contact. Charles Wellbeloved was now seventy and John Kenrick had resigned on account of ill-health in 1839. It was felt that Manchester was the true home for the College and, when put to the vote, this was agreed.

The new Principal was to be the Reverend Robert Wallace, a contemporary of John Robberds at York, and John Robberds was appointed Professor of pastoral Theology and Hebrew and John Tayler Professor of Ecclesiastical History, both men continuing their ministerial duties. Among other professors appointed were John Kenrick and James Martineau, each remaining resident in his home at York and at Liverpool, and coming over to Manchester for their lectures. William Gaskell was appointed clerical secretary and worked in close partnership with the law secretary, his friend Samuel Dukinfield Darbyshire, a successful Manchester solicitor, and a loyal and faithful member of Cross Street Chapel.

The College was housed in a building in the heart of Manchester near All Saints Church in the former home of the influential Marsland family, where there was accommodation for a common hall and library. The course of studies continued to be as at York, of three years for lay students and five for divinity. Students were housed in lodgings approved by the trustees and were worked hard. They missed the community life that students had enjoyed at York but appreciated the welcome they received on regular visits to the Robberds and Gaskell homes. In later life one student recalled the country walks they sometimes took in Mrs Gaskell's company and the Shakespearean evenings with Mr Robberds. They returned this hospitality by inviting ministers and their wives to tea in the college library.

In 1846 John Kenrick became Principal upon Robert Wallace's retirement and William was appointed in his place as Professor of History, Literature and Logic. He thus became one of the College's team of dedicated teachers and thinkers who did so much to restore to Unitarianism the spiritual aspect that since

Priestley's time had been overshadowed by rationalism. John Tayler and James Martineau were the most passionate advocates of the new attitudes and as tutors of divinity and philosophy made their influence felt. William, by virtue of his reserved nature, played a more supportive role, concentrating his energies on the subjects he was teaching and inspiring his students with a love of the English language, and winning their respect and affection. His lectures were always well attended and like his sermons these were carefully prepared and delivered in his clear musical voice.

The same year that he became tutor discussions were started on the College's future, following two events that opened up

24. All Saints Church, mid-nineteenth century.

wider educational opportunities for Dissenters. In 1844, the Dissenters' Chapel Act had given legislative recognition to unlimited religious liberty and two years later University Hall was established in Gordon Square, London, associated with University College, to provide for the teaching of theology and mental and moral philosophy, and open to both nonconformists and members of the Established Church. Also in 1846, in Manchester, John Owens, a local business man left a bequest of £97,000 for the benefit of instructing young men in 'such branches of science and learning as are usually taught in English universities without any test of religious opinions'. It was evident that Manchester New College's true function was now as a School of Theology attached either to University College or to Owens' College. The decision to move the College to London was not reached until 1853 after long deliberation, by which time University Hall and Owens' College were firmly established. Sixty students had passed through the College during the thirteen years in Manchester, thirty-two trained as divinity and twenty-eight as lay students.

John Tayler was appointed as the first Principal in London and was reluctant to leave Manchester where he had his roots. He was anxious for James Martineau to share the teaching with him and after a year his former colleague was appointed as a visiting lecturer, travelling down from Liverpool once a fortnight. In 1856 there was a vacancy for a full-time tutor and a special committee was set up by the college trustees under the chairmanship of William Gaskell, to consider the appointment of Dr Martineau to this position. This chairmanship called for all William's tact and diplomacy as there was some divergence of opinion among committee members, the older Unitarians considering that Martineau was an unwelcome innovator. At a meeting in January 1857 William read a letter from Tayler embodying proposals for the sharing of teaching between himself and Martineau and offering to resign if necessary. Tayler referred to Martineau as 'the man whose writings are more widely read by the thoughtful and inquiring of all parties than those of any other of our body'. This proposal was accepted by fourteen to five; but the opponents collected over sixty signatures from others of their opinion and published a protest on the grounds that views deemed by many Unitarians to be essential to Christian truth would be shut

25. James Martineau, 1888, from an engraving of the portrait by
G.F. Watts.

out from the instruction given by Tayler and Martineau. The committee made a further report and finally in April the college trustees gave a vote of confidence in favour of Tayler and Martineau sharing the teaching. At this meeting the original principle established at Warrington Academy and later absorbed by William under Charles Wellbeloved at York was once again affirmed, that the College was founded for the sole purpose of giving university learning to students to the Christian ministry, not for the purpose of instruction in the peculiar doctrines of any sect. William must have gained much satisfaction from having presided over these deliberations and the happy outcome.

After the College moved to London William Gaskell still retained close ties, remaining as Chairman of the committee and serving as Visitor from 1859 until the end of his life. Twenty years later he was once again in the position of Chairman when discussions were held on yet another move for this College, this time to Oxford. On that occasion he moved the resolution that the College remain in London, but at the same time avowed his own preference for its return to Manchester if practicable. He did not however live to see its removal to Oxford in 1888.

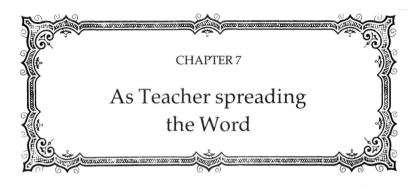

CHAPTER 7

As Teacher spreading the Word

John Robberds died in 1854 and William Gaskell became senior minister at Cross Street. It would have been understandable if with the assumption of his new duties, he had felt glad to be relieved of his teaching commitments at New College. Any relaxation of effort was, however, contrary to his nature and that same year he entered wholeheartedly into plans set in motion by his friend Dr John Relly Beard for the establishment of a new training centre in Manchester specifically for Unitarian ministers. The aim was to provide opportunities to train for the ministry men with non-academic backgrounds, including those past the first flush of youth, who felt called to serve Unitarian Churches. More men were needed as ministers in the already established chapels, and also to revive those whose support was lacking, and to found new ones. More ministers were required to further the work of the Manchester Domestic Mission among the city's growing population.

The new training centre was to be called the Unitarian Home Missionary Board, the name emphasising the fact that one of its prime objects was to equip men to go out and spread the faith. Both Dr Beard and William Gaskell knew from their experience that the Unitarian faith was particularly fitting to the needs of working men and women because of the simplicity of its message and its freedom from dogma. They knew too that the message would best be received from men not raised from the richer and more educated classes of society, as were many of the clergy. Although himself an academic, William had acquired the common touch and had already won the hearts of Manchester's people in all walks of life, through his work in chapel and Sunday school and meeting them in their homes and inviting them to his. Dr Beard too had lived and worked in Strangeways for over twenty years, had run a private school and taught English, Greek and Latin by correspondence. Both men were admirably equipped to train as their pupils men who had been called to serve as Unitarian ministers.

The decision to form the Home Missionary Board was made at a meeting in Cross Street Chapel Room on 31 May 1854, Dr Beard being appointed Principal and tutor in theology and William Gaskell tutor in literature, history and New Testament Greek. Ten students were enrolled, varying in age from nineteen to thirty-eight, not all Unitarians born and bred, and men who had been in such occupations as clerk, printer, watchmaker, warehouseman and silk weaver. The first term started in December with an inaugural service at Cross Street Chapel where the two tutors gave addresses. Dr Beard spoke on the necessity for missionary effort and William on the course of studies to be followed. 'Be furnished with the best implements', he said, and stressed the need to speak out in clear, sharp and fitting words with 'truth and force' on the importance of God's message. He spoke of language as being a great gift that God had 'fearfully and wonderfully made'. The study of literature would enable students to use language perfectly; the study of Greek would bring freshness to Biblical passages that had lost some of their meaning through long familiarity.

It was round the table in William Gaskell's study at Plymouth Grove that his students received their first lessons, as the Home Missionary Board had no premises for the first six months. Dr Beard also held his lectures in his home in Lower Broughton. Once a week William used the Cross Street Chapel Room for lectures and students were granted use of the Chapel library. In August 1855, three rooms were found in premises at 102 Cross Street. Students were lodged in rooms in the town and received a bursary of 10s., but as rents ran to 4s. a week without light and heating there was little left for food after buying books and candles. The full training was spread over three years, of two terms a year, and much emphasis was placed on preparing students to assist ministers in neighbouring chapels with preaching, teaching and visiting. The mornings were devoted to lectures while the afternoons and evenings were given over to

26. William Gaskell, a plaque found at Cross Street Chapel.

the more practical side of their training when they went out on pastoral visits and to Sunday schools, mission halls and chapels. Much attention was given to the preparation and delivery of sermons; their schemes and outlines on set texts were criticised, and elocution and reading aloud were included in their studies. Public examinations largely oral, were first held in Cross Street Chapel and students preached a test sermon in Dr Beard's chapel at Bridge Street, Strangeways. The success of this curriculum was proved by figures published for the 1858-9 session when students had taken over 1,000 services in 64 different places of worship.

In 1857 the Board found slightly larger premises with four rooms at the top of an old warehouse in Marsden Square, but these were very inadequate. William is quoted as saying: 'I liked the Board very much but not the lodging'. His cousin Holbrook, who was president of the Board in 1862, was dismayed when he visited these quarters. He described how he climbed up 'the winding creaking stairs' to the attic at the top of 'a mean and sordid pile of buildings'; when he opened the door he saw 'a number of men seated round some tables who seemed to be more like a band of conspirators concealed from the eyes of the police than our large-hearted earnest members of the Home Missionary Board'. Mrs Gaskell too was concerned at the conditions in which William and his students had to work. She wrote to a friend: 'He had three days of four hours each at the Home Missionary Board and that in a very close room which added to the fatigue'.

During the early years of the Board Adam Rushton, a working man from Macclesfield, was a student. He wrote many interesting reminiscences of his years in Manchester in his book *My Life as Farmer's Boy, Factoryhand, Teacher and Preacher'*. He became a student in 1856 at the age of thirty-three, having been a Sunday school teacher in Macclesfield since boyhood, and, while employed as a silk weaver, became converted to Unitarianism. He described his attendance at the Board's entrance examination when he had to write a sermon on a set text while 'professors walked about the room', but he added 'the atmosphere was pleasant'. A viva voce examination followed and at the end of the day he was told he was accepted. He wrote of the lectures he attended at Dr Beard's which he found too discursive, but when he went to Mr Gaskell's house in Plymouth Grove for three or four hours of concentrated study he found his tutor's 'pleasant method of teaching helped me to bear the strain'. The reading of *Paradise Lost* with his comments and questions was 'an inspiration'; and he added 'to hear Mr Gaskell read and pronounce Greek was a delicious pleasure'. He referred to the lighthearted manner in which the tutor commented on his students' extempore addresses and criticised them with plenty of good humour.

Rushton described his final test, when he had to deliver an address in Manchester Town Hall at the Annual General Meeting of the Home Missionary Board. The Hall was crowded and he felt very nervous, but gained confidence as he spoke. He reviewed all he had learnt during his three year course and paid tribute to William Gaskell with these words: 'With Mr Gaskell I had had many delightful experiences. In his company I had visited the seers and sages of Greece and Rome; had become familiar with great statesmen, warriors and scholars of ancient times; had made close acquaintance with the persons and writings of England's greatest literary men; had passed from the times of Merlin the Enchanter to the time of Caedmon and Chaucer, on to the age of Shakespeare and Milton and down to the distinguished scholars of the present time'.He noticed that Mrs Gaskell was in the audience, sitting on a form in front and was intensely amused when he introduced some touches of humour.

After his training Adam Rushton became minister at Padiham where his two tutors preached at his induction, John Beard on the duties of a minister and William Gaskell on the duties of a congregation, and both welcomed him in affectionate terms to the ministry. In 1862 he was urged by these two men to take over important work for the Manchester District Unitarian Missionary Association that had been formed in 1859. For five years he worked at Blackley and was sole superintendent of six missionary stations in surrounding towns. Adam Rushton is typical of the students who emerged from the Home Missionary Board to play a vital part in the spread of Unitarianism in Man--chester and beyond.

It was remarkable that such a small group of people meeting in such cramped quarters could wield so much influence. In 1862 steps were taken by William Gaskell and John Beard to improve their accommodation. This was the bicentenary year of the event spoken of by Dissenters as the Great Ejection of 1662. To mark the occasion they set plans afoot to raise finance for a building for the Home Missionary Board. A site was found in Albert Square and plans were drawn up for a spacious assembly hall, committee rooms and a library. William Gaskell and John Beard devised a circular giving notice of a meeting to open the fund and referred to the debt owed to their forebears, 'the two thousand godly ministers ejected from the Established Church, who are our spiritual forefathers and to whose example and influence religious freedom and earnest piety we are under great and lasting obligation.'

Funds gradually accumulated, including £543 from past students, and the foundation stone was laid in 1864. The hall subsequently known as the Memorial Hall was opened the following year. William continued as tutor at the Board until the end of his life, succeeding John Beard as Principal in 1878.

It seems as though he found his greatest fulfilment in teaching and never spared himself. 'You may have only one talent but you dare not bury it', he had told the students of the Home Missionary Board at the inaugural address and his own gift as a teacher he share liberally. He found time to take classes in literature at a Working Men's College started in Manchester in 1858 in which he collaborated with Alexander Scott, a close friend, who, like William, had been giving lectures at working men's clubs for many years. The College meeting place was the Mechanics' Institution in David Street, where lectures were held each evening for two hours. Students had to be aged sixteen or over, and able to read and write and had to pass a simple entrance examination. They were required to pay a fee of half a crown a term of ten weeks, except for Bible-reading classes held on Sunday afternoons, which were free. The lecturers gave their services free. William Gaskell was on the board of management and took the English literature class one evening a week. 193 students were enrolled for the first term at the College and this increased to 203 in the second term. William's classes attracted the highest number of students, 87 in the first term, and maintained the best attendance figures in the College, having an average of 63 regularly present. Mr Scott took classes in political philosophy and, after his appointment as Principal of Owens' College, the Working Men's College was incorporated into evening classes there from 1861. In 1863 William took over Mr Scott's classes in logic during a period of illness. His work at the College involved him in 'two long hours' two evenings a week, as Elizabeth complained in a letter to Ann Robson, in 1865, and 'on Monday evening too', she continued, 'which is often a hard day with committees etc., but you might as well ask St Paul's to tumble down as to entreat him to give up this piece of work which does interest him very much and which no one could do so well, certainly, only it does come at such an unlucky time'.

Many tributes were paid to their teacher by his working men pupils. One of them, Mr W.E. Adams in his book, *Memoirs of a Social Atom* of 1903 wrote: 'Mr Gaskell was a master of literature and I thought at the time he was the most beautiful reader I have ever heard. Prose and poetry seemed to acquire a new lustre and elegance when he read it. Our literary evenings with Mr Gaskell were ambrosial evenings indeed'.

Another former student, Mr Wright, in his reminiscences *Young Days* gave two examples of William's ability to handle a class with the right combination of severity and humour:

One morning before Mr Gaskell came into the lecture room, the students became somewhat lively. Perhaps it was cold and they wanted exercise! However it was, a few leathern cushion from the chairs got flying about. The bell rang, signal for the

27. The Mechanics' Institute, David Street, Manchester.

incoming of Mr Gaskell. There was hurry and scurry to get all the cushions on the chairs again. The door from his room into the lecture-room opened a few inches - he was coming - when a flying cushion hit it and slammed the door *to* again. There was silence, and every student was gravely seated when Mr Gaskell with quiet dignity appeared, and significantly said 'Gentlemen! Gentlemen! If I may say *gentlemen!*' Not another word was said or needed.

But the best story of all - and well known among his old students - is one which shows the *readiness* of Mr Gaskell's mind. One day Mr Gaskell happened to seat himself in a chair whose joints were very loose. He crossed his legs as usual, opened his book, and called upon Mr So-and-So to begin reading. Before this young gentleman had read very far he made a regular 'howler' of a mistake. Mr Gaskell sprang from his seat (whether in real or partly affected amazement, I do not know) but as he sprang up, the chair fell to pieces on the floor, and Mr Gaskell, looking first behind him in surprise as he stood there, now looked at the blundering student and exclaimed, 'Mr So-and-So, *the very chair can't stand it!*'

Others who admitted owing a great deal to William's teaching were the Winkworth sisters who came to him for private lessons in a variety of subjects and later became intimate friends of the whole Gaskell family. There were five daughters, Emily, **Susanna, Catherine, Selina and Alice who were in their late teens and twenties** when they started lessons from him in history, composition and chemistry while the Gaskells were still at Dover Street. Their own family life was disrupted by the death of their mother and after their father's re-marriage Susanna and Catherine went abroad to study German and art in Geneva. On their return they began Greek lessons with William and at this time met Elizabeth and found in the Gaskell houehold all the warmth and love lacking in their own home and remained friends for life. They became very much part of the Gaskell circle, sharing a common interest in literature, languages, music and art, taking an active part in social work at Cross Street, though not themselves Unitarians. Catherine and Susanna both worked on German translations with William's help. Through the Gaskells they met the German scholar and statesman Chevalier Bunsen who had made a collection of nine hundred hymns.

Under William's guidance Catherine worked on a translation of nearly a hundred of these hymns that were published in 1853 under the title *Lyra Germanica,* the best known being 'Now thank we all our God' and 'Praise to the Lord the Almighty the King of Creation'. William was very meticulous and she told her sister that Mr Gaskell found out no end of faults for her to corect. Susanna wrote a life of the German historian, Barthold Niebuhr (1776-1831) and William was checking the proofs at the same time as Elizabeth was working on *Mary Barton.* She commented on this fact in a letter to her friend Eliza Fox in 1851: 'Susanna W. keeps Wm. busy at work correcting her proofs, for my dear! Niebuhr is on the point of appearing before the public! and poor Mary Barton gets more snubbed than ever as "light and transitory".' The book came out in 1852 and Elizabeth wrote in a light-hearted and non-malicious way to the same friend 'I wish you could see S.W. she is so funny and cock a hoop about Niebuhr, she snubs me so and makes such love to William he says "my life is the only protection he has - else he *knows* she would marry him". I wish you could hear him speaking thus in a meek fatalist kind of way, and I believe she *would* too'. Obviously William found the devotion of the two sisters something of an embarrassment. But it was admiration and respect that they felt for him and they acknowledged the debt that they owed him for the stimulation they received from his lessons.

Other private pupils were Maggie Leisler, one of the daughters of a Manchester merchant and his wife whom the Gaskells met socially, and Mary Stewart who later, as Mrs Molesworth, became a successful writer of popular children's books. She came with her parents to live in Dover Street in 1853 when she was a child and started lessons with William Gaskell, then at Plymouth Grove. She left Manchester after her marriage and several of her books were published during William's life time, *Carrots, just a Little Boy* in 1870, *The Cuckoo Clock* in 1877, *The Tapestry Room* in 1879. She was describing the Manchester that the Gaskells knew in her book *The Carved Lions* when she wrote of 'a rather large town in an ugly part of the country where great tall chimneys giving out black smoke and steam, and streams whose waters were nearly as black as the smoke, made it often difficult to believe in blue sky or green grass, or any of the sweet pure country scenes that children love'. If he had read this

William would have taken pride and pleasure in seeing how his lessons had borne fruit.

Time was always made for his own daughters' lessons and even after they had been away to school, they turned to him for advice on their reading when they returned home. When he and Elizabeth agreed to let Marianne take on the lessons of her two youngest sisters in 1852 William set aside two periods a week for reading with her, to continue her own education. He always seemed able to expand his time and to give generously the fruits of his richly stored mind.

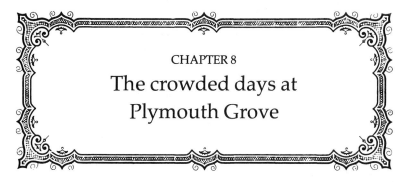

CHAPTER 8

The crowded days at
Plymouth Grove

By the time William was appointed senior minister at Cross Street Chapel in 1854 Elizabeth had been contributing stories to Charles Dickens' magazine *Household Words* for four years, including *Cranford* in weekly instalments, and had completed her second novel *Ruth* in 1852. The Gaskells were entering a phase in their lives when each would be under the pressure of conflicting loyalties, so many demands being made upon their time and energies. They had no doubts as to where their priorities lay; with William his vocation as preacher and teacher had to come before his role as husband and father: with Elizabeth home duties and charitable works must supersede her literary work and social life. Both, however, were flexible in the conduct of their daily lives and worked in harmony so that William readily assumed resonsibility of the household when Elizabeth's health or literary commitments necessitated her being away from Manchester: Elizabeth took over much of her husband's visiting and entertaining of chapel friends to set him free for more pressing claims.

In 1850 they decided to move from Upper Rumford Street into a larger house. Their financial circumstances had improved since William's appointment as tutor at Manchester New College, and Elizabeth's earnings as a writer were increasing. In addition she received a second legacy from Aunt Lumb's estate, following the death of her aunt Abigail Holland, when the girlhood home at Knutsford was sold. William and Elizabeth found just the house they wanted at 42 Plymouth Grove, not far from Rumford Street, but at that time, as its name suggested, a leafy district with open fields near at hand and a sizeable garden. Elizabeth at first had a few qualms of conscience about 'spending so much on *so* purely selfish a thing as a house is when so many are wanting', as she wrote to her friend Eliza Fox, but admitted to being 'highly delighted at the delight of everyone else in the house, Meta and William most especially are in full ecstasy'. She tried to justify herself by saying 'It is Wm. who is to decide on all these things and his feeling it right ought to be my rule and so it is - only that does not quite do. Well, I must try and make the house give as much pleasure to others as I can and made it as little a selfish thing as I can'. And so it proved.

The removal to their new home heralded the beginning of the crowded years for both of them and the in-comings and out-goings at Plymouth Grove could be likened to the activities of a beehive. They had come a long way since the simple house at Dover Street where they had required only the services of the servant Betsy, until the babies were born. At Rumford Street Ann Hearn joined them and remained with the family for fifty years, always referred to as Hearn who became the 'dear good valuable friend' that Elizabeth described her and someone with whom she and William were happy to trust the care of the girls when little, and their chaperone on their travels as they grew older. More domestic staff were needed at 42 Plymouth Grove, where there were seven bedrooms, two attics, three living rooms and kitchen premises in the basement. They took on a cook and several maids, at one time employing a staff of five including a man for outside work, and also using the services of a washer-woman and sempstress. Although relieved of many domestic tasks Elizabeth never relinquished the running of the household and worked in close harmony with the staff, training them well and taking a keen interest in their welfare. It is perhaps some-times forgotten that the Victorians who employed young domestic staff took on serious responsibilities, standing *in loco parentis*. William and Elizabeth were exemplary employers, taking a close interest in the personal problems of those who worked for them, readily granting leave of absence so that they could go home at times of family crises, and in 1851 their cook Mary was married by 'the Master'. Once Elizabeth was estab-lished as an authoress and was earning money from her books she travelled a great deal with her daughters to further their education and it was imperative to have trustworth servants to

28. The Gaskells' house in Plymouth Grove (now no.84) William lived here from 1850 until his death in 1884.

keep the household running smoothly for William while she was away and his chapel duties kept him in Manchester. Of necessity their scale of entertaining increased in frequency and in numbers of visitors, so domestic help was essential. Their style of life was gradually changing and perhaps they sometimes looked back with nostalgia to the informalities of their early married life, such as the occasion when they thought nothing of walking, Elizabeth in great thick shoes and William in boots and without gloves, to a christening party in north Manchester, walking back home in daylight at 3.30a.m., as she described in a letter in midsummer 1838.

They never lost touch with friends of earlier days, among them the now venerable William Turner and Rosa Mitchell, former governess to the girls. Old Mr Turner, who had been Elizabeth's mentor and teacher during her stay in Newcastle upon Tyne in her girlhood, and the respected Visitor at Manchester New College, York, during William's student days, had christened Margaret Emily when they visited him in 1837. He had remained minister at Hanover Square Chapel, Newcastle, for fifty-eight years and his work there closely paralleled William's in Manchester. Mr Turner worked tirelessly to lighten the lot of the poor, especially in the field of education, establishing the first Sunday School in the north-east of England. He ran a school of his own for a number of years and taught George Stephenson when he was an obscure workman; he served as secretary to both the Newcastle Literary and Philosophical Society, which he founded, and the British and Foreign Bible Society; he was in great demand as a lecturer.

William Turner came to Manchester on his retirement in 1841 and lived with his daughter Ann, near the Robberds in Greenheys, then after her death, with Rosa Mitchell. Mrs Gaskell used to call regularly at Miss Mitchell's to read to Mr Turner when his sight was going. When the old man died at the age of ninety-eight William preached the funeral sermon at Cross Street Chapel. He chose as his text 'Thou shalt go to thy father in peace; thou shalt be buried in a good old age'. He spoke of William Turner's work in Newcastle and of his delight in doing good. William referred to the sound practical advice that Turner had always given in his addresses at Manchester New College. 'He was no bigoted sectarian', said William, and went on to quote a remark made about his friend that a lady had made in his defence, when the minister of an Established Church had suggested that she could not expect to see Mr Turner, a Unitarian, in Heaven. 'No, I confess I do not', the lady replied, 'He will be too much in the light of the throne for me to see him'.

Elizabeth was working on her novel *Ruth* during the years that she was visiting Mr Turner at Miss Mitchell's and the old man was still alive when the book was published in 1852 so it is possible that she could have read some of it aloud to him. He would have been too modest to have recognised himself in the character of Thurstan Benson in the novel, whom Elizabeth endowed with those qualities of a practical Christian that she and William most admired and which their friend possessed in full measure.

An example of the Gaskells' own practical Christianity is shown in the steps they took for the welfare of Miss Mitchell, prior to Mr Turner's death. Rosa was suffering from a heart condition and was to some extent dependent on the money she received from her lodger. Foreseeing his imminent death the

Gaskells arranged for a fund to be started to which mutual friends would contribute to ensure that Rosa Mitchell would be relieved of financial anxiety. A letter which Elizabeth wrote in February 1856 to remind one of the contributors that his payment was due contains this sentence:

'Mr Gaskell thought it better to place the whole matter at once on a business footing and to pay her £12. 10s. quarterly, which he has done; and I do believe if you could all know how much you have done to smooth away a very natural care and anxiety from the last years of as good and Christian a woman as ever was, you would be very much touched and grateful'.

At Plymouth Grove they had their own pony and chaise and this necessitated the employment of a man who combined the care of the horse, Tommy, and the carriage, with outside work in the garden. William often drove the children out with Tommy and when the family were holidaying at Silverdale, they hired a carriage. Catherine Winkworth described a happy occasion when she was staying with the Gaskells at their holiday home when a sketching party was arranged at the village of Clapham. She and Marianne had gone on in advance to find accommodation while William drove the rest of the party over and 'did not arrive until late, but when they did their cool moonlight drive over the moors had put them in high spirits and we were all a very jolly party over a magnificent tea'.

Rosa Mitchell was one of their friends who was always a welcome visitor at Silverdale. She was someone with whom both could feel completely at ease at their holiday retreat, Elizabeth making the most of the opportunities to write, and William enjoying the atmosphere of informality. They first stayed at Silverdale for six weeks in 1850 and fell in love with the place. Elizabeth described it to a friend in these words: 'Silverdale is hardly to be called the seaside as it is a little dale running down to Morecambe Bay, with grey limestone rocks on all sides, which in the sun or moonlight glisten like silver. And we are keeping holiday in the most unusual farmhouse lodgings so that the children learn country interests and ways of living'. This was written from Lindeth Farm where they were accommodated in the farmhouse, but on future holdiays they stayed at Lindeth Lodge, which they spoke of as the Wolf House because a wolf figures in the heraldic device over the door, and then at Lindeth

Tower, a stone-built folly erected by a retired Preston banker in 1842. This building was four storeys high with a single room on each landing. Elizabeth used the room on the top floor for her writing where, according to farm workers, she was seen at work in the early morning as they were on their way to the fields. 'One is never disappointed in coming back to Silverdale', she wrote, 'the secret is the expanse of view'.

'Papa likes the idea of Silverdale' she wrote in 1852, when plans for their holiday were being made. Three years later when William was planning a holiday walking with a friend in Switzerland she wrote on the eve of his departure that before setting off ' he wants to hear of our safe arrival at Silverdale'.

After the peace of their holidays the Gaskells returned refreshed to the bustle of life at Plymouth Grove where friends and visitors were always made to feel at home. This was in large measure due to Elizabeth's natural charm and high spirits. William was less at ease in the company of strangers and although spoken of as a fine conversationalist with a fund of appropriate anecdotes when in the company of his family, colleagues and friends, was not so adept at 'small talk' with casual acquaintances. Much can be learnt from Elizabeth's letters of life at Plymouth Grove and it is from them one can gain an insight into the pattern of life there and the home background into which William had to fit his absorbing duties of minister and teacher. Reading between the lines of her letters something of William's attitudes and behaviour during these crowded years can be surmised, but of necessity because of lack of his own letters what follows must be largely conjecture.

William must often have felt oppressed by the bustling female household with wife, daughters, maidservants, Sunday School girls, women callers, sewing parties and charity committees. He probably found the chatter of some of Elizabeth's women friends tedious, but he approved wholeheartedly of the Winkworth sisters and of Eliza Fox, daughter of William Fox, journalist and Member of Parliament, to whom Elizabeth wrote that William had remarked: 'It is not often I make such a suitable friendship as the one with you'. To the same friend Elizabeth commented in a letter during a busy week in October 1852, with company in the house, that William was 'too busy to be agreeable to my unfortunate visitors and I had to do double duty'. Several years later she wrote to Marianne: 'Papa has been too busy to be talked to and today is quite unapproachable'.

Elizabeth understood William's need for quiet and privacy to work on his sermons, lectures and lessons and protected him from visitors as best she could. She confessed to feeling embarrassed when she heard the tea bell rung on Saturday afternoons and was never able to invite a young engineering apprentice, Fleming Jenkin, who called regularly on that day to see the family, to stay to tea. Saturday evenings were sacrosanct as William would be putting the finishing touches to the next day's sermons; sometimes he would be preaching at three services on the Sunday and would work until midnight copying them out.

William had again to excuse himself from such an interesting visitor as Lowes Dickenson, a portrait painter, who called on them in 1860. His visit was referred to by Elizabeth as a real pleasure, but 'Mr Gaskell however missed his share owing to his inevitable Saturday night's sermon, but he hopes Mr Dickenson will come and see us again when he returns to Manchester and then Mr Gaskell will make up for lost time'. William's study, to which he so often retreated, and his favourite room in the house, was a book-lined room situated to the right of the square entrance hall immediately inside the double doors through which the house was entered from the handsome columned porch. Being so located the study was immediately accessible to his visiting students coming for weekly lessons and the constant stream of chapel and college associates and Manchester businessmen, scientists and philanthropists with whom he served on countless committees. On the other side of the front door was the morning room used as the girls' schoolroom and at the far end of the hall, framed by an archway, lay the drawing room and dining room joined by connecting doors on the left, and a staircase rose to the right. This was the domain of the family where social calls were received, and where Elizabeth did her writing on the dining room table at the hub of the household; but round this same table she and William entertained many famous visitors who sat and dined, as Charlotte Bronte wrote, off 'Mrs Gaskell's beautiful Minton dinner service', or breakfasted 'off her Coalport ware'. Elizabeth and William loved beautiful things around them but added treasures to their home sparingly, savouring the excitement of each new acquisition. In 1851

Elizabeth told her sister-in-law, Anne Robson, that the house was proving expensive and with Marianne's school fees to be paid they had decided not to furnish the drawing room. But as the years passed they picked up 'little bits of prettiness' when they could afford them but 'were not rich enough to make great changes' she wrote to her American friend Charles Norton in 1859. In 1851 Elizabeth was pleased to come across a second-hand library desk in London for William's study - and in 1852 they made an extravagant but essential purchase of a semi-grand Broadwood piano. Of equal pleasure to them as such material acquisitions was the possession of the large garden. William bought a second hand garden frame where they could harden off plants for bedding out and they went in for a far larger variety of vegetables than the celery that wanted earthing up at Dover Street while they were on their honeymoon. There was a conservatory, too, at Plymouth Grove, so no need to put saucers under the plants on the window sill as in those early days. In 1851 Elizabeth wrote to Marianne: 'I think Papa enjoys the garden more than ever this year. he and Meta are constantly out of doors'. Elizabeth, remembering the joys of the garden at Knutsford, wanted to emulate Aunt Lumb, so they rented a field adjoining the garden and kept their own cow, a pig and some chickens, but this seemed to be her responsibility and not William's.

His workshop was his study and here he was continually at his desk engaged in much secretarial and committee work beyond his essential chapel and college duties. He was gravely concerned with the living conditions of Manchester's poor and the danger to health caused by overcrowding and poor sanitation. He worked for the Manchester and Salford Sanitary Association set up to combat the threat of cholera, and served on the committee from 1852, lecturing during the 1854-5 session on 'The Transgression of the Laws of Health'. He served on a committee set up in 1852 to work for the better regulation of beer houses and places of entertainment. These interests brought him in touch with many of Manchester's most public-spirited citizens and he numbered among his friends men who became mayors of Manchester, Sir John Potter and his brother Thomas, and Sir Thomas Baker, a stalwart of Cross Street Chapel. Mark Philips, Manchester's first Member of Parliament, and his brother Robert, the

Member for Bury, were also among his friends. A Liberal at heart William never openly declared his allegiance to any political party and never lent his name nor gave financial support to the Free Trade movement of which many of his friends were ardent supporters. His wife summed up his attitude in a letter to Marianne in 1852: 'Speechmaking, public meetings and such noisy obtrusive ways of "doing good" are his dislike, as you know, but oh! he is so good really in his own quiet way, beginning at home and working outwards without noise or hubbub - I am more and more convinced *be* good and *doing* comes naturally and need not be fussed or spoken about'.

The occasion that prompted this comment was an invitation that William had received from the British Association for the Advancement of Science of which he was a member, to give a lecture at their meeting in London. It was the size and importance of the meeting of which Elizabeth said, 'he lived in dread'. However, two years later the Association's meeting was held in Liverpool, where he was on home ground, and gave one of his lectures on Lancashire dialect, and eleven years later had no qualms about going to London to give a set of lectures on this, his favourite topic, to the Royal Institute. Two of the Gaskells' oldest friends were engineers and also members of the British Association. William Fairbairn with engineering works in Manchester, and James Nasmyth,. inventor of the steam hammer, who was in partnership with William's cousin, Holbrook Gaskell, controlling the Bridgewater Foundry in Manchester, were regular visitors with their wives to Plymouth Grove. Elizabeth based one of the characters in her book *Cousin Phillis* on James Nasmyth, an engineering genius who learnt his skills in the workshop. Mr Manning, the engineer in the novel, is described as 'a man in decent but unfashionable Sunday clothes, his plain sensible face full of hard lines - the marks of toil and thought - his hands blackened beyond the power of soap and water by years of labour in the foundry, speaking with a strong Northern dialect'. Such a man was Nasmyth.

These were people with whom William and Elizabeth were very much at ease and shared many common interests. Fairbairn, later Sir William, was a member and, at one period, President of the Manchester Literary and Philosophical Society. He read Elizabeth's novels and made helpful comments on those passages in them that dealt with the relationships between masters and men. These were friends with whom the Gaskells attended the many public lectures that were held in Manchester at that time by such celebrities as John Ruskin, Charles Dickens and William Makepeace Thackeray, whom they also met at social gatherings. The Gaskells were also concert-goers and attended the concerts under Charles Hallé that were started during the Great Masters Art Exhibition in Manchester in 1857. The exhibition ran for five and a half months and attracted over a million visitors to see the paintings, sculpture, furniture and ceramics on display, in a special building erected in Old Trafford and visited by Queen Victoria.

During the run of the Exhibition the comings and goings at Plymouth Grove were hectic. Elizabeth wrote to Eliza Fox on 26 August: 'We have two rooms and nineteen people coming to occupy them before the Exhibition closes... We are worn out with hospitality... I should like it dearly if I weren't a hostess'. She quoted some remarks of Marianne's in a letter to Charles Norton a month later which shows her to be her father's own daughter. 'Oh! are you not tired of being agreeable? I do so want leisure to sulk and be silent in', the girl complained. Perhaps William was too much in control of his feelings to sulk but he certainly needed the silence of his study.

29. The Great Masters Art Exhibition, Manchester, 1857.

1857 was a particularly difficult year for the Gaskells as this was the year that saw the publication of Elizabeth's *Life of Charlotte Brontë* by Smith, Elder & Co. This book followed her novel *North and South* which was serialised in *Household Words*. It was work she had undertaken at the request of the Reverend Patrick Brontë who knew how valued a friend Elizabeth had become after the meeting of the two women novelists in 1850. Elizabeth received much practical help from her family during her two years work on the book. William accepted without demur her many absences from home while engaged on research and found time to read her manuscript and check the proofs. 'I have not such a keen eye for typographical errors as Mr Gaskell', she told her publisher. Marianne and Meta copied out for their mother many of Charlotte's letters lent by friends.

As soon as the book was finished in the February of 1857 William encouraged Elizabeth to take a holiday in Italy with the two older girls. He knew her need for rest and change and her dislike of the publicity attendant upon the publication of each new book from this now popular author. She received no news of the uproar that the *Life* caused in some quarters and did not return home until William and Mr Shaen had pacified those who were threatening legal action. In spite of the fact that William had shouldered the responsibility and silenced the critics Elizabeth was extremely shaken by the whole experience. 'I have cried more since I came home than I ever did in the same space of time before and never needed kind words so much - and no one gives me them', she wrote. Perhaps William felt that sympathy was not the answer, and this is borne out in a letter written five days later when Elizabeth said 'You can't think how kindness touches me just now; almost painfully'. Perhaps the arrival of guests for the Exhibition was just what was needed to turn her thoughts in other directions.

Another occurrence served to focus the attention of William and Elizabeth in an unexpected quarter in the summer of that year. This was the sudden engagement of Meta, then twenty years old, to Captain Charles Hill, an officer in the Indian Army, on leave in England, whom she had met two years previously. His regiment was to be recalled and they hoped to marry immediately, so that Meta could return to India with him. William and Elizabeth dreaded the thought of being separated from their daughter by such a distance but put no obstacle in her way. Fortunately the marriage was postponed, in view of the unsettled situation in India after the Mutiny, and it was arranged that Meta should go out the following year to Egypt where Charles would join her for the wedding. In the spring of 1859 Meta broke off the engagement because of adverse facts that came to her knowledge about her fiancé. Her parents were profoundly relieved, though distressed for Meta. It appears that William may have always had reservations about Captain Hill, as Elizabeth confided to her friend, Ellen Nussey, while the engagement was on, that 'Mr Gaskell never names his name'.

Elizabeth took the girls off to their beloved Silverdale after the engagement was broken off and in the autumn of 1858 they went to Heidelberg while William went on a walking tour with his brother Sam. This had become the pattern of their holidays by the time the girls were old enough to enjoy travel and there was money to spare to take them abroad. He could not easily be persuaded to leave Manchester to join them abroad and in any case preferred 'to bachelorise off', as Elizabeth termed it, with a male companion. He made the most of the opportunity for exercise and freedom from formality that a walking holiday provided, and was able to relax completely when he was away in places where he was not known and could escape from the strait-lacing imposed by Victorians on ministers of the church. When they were apart William and Elizabeth regularly exchanged letters, as is confirmed by references in her letters to her daughters, but none of these letters has survived. A hint of feelings about holidays was given when Marianne wanted a friend to join the family at Silverdale in 1852. Elizabeth wrote to her: 'Papa does not like the idea of having a stranger in the house at holiday time, when you know he likes to play pranks and go cockling etc. etc. and feels at liberty to say and do what he likes... Papa would feel constrained and obliged to be proper'. He usually spent part of his month's leave of absence from the Chapel with the family if they were holidaying in Britain, and then fitted in some weeks on his own according to their plans, on several occasions going walking with the Unitarian minister at Bristol, his friend the Reverend William James. Elizabeth was delighted when he and Mr James went off to Switzerland in 1856 and bought him a new waterproof overcoat for the occasion. He often

30. William Gaskell on holiday in Scotland, from a photograph by Rupert Potter, Beatrix Potter's father.

joined Edmund Potter and his family at the holiday home they took each year in Wales, the Lakes or Scotland. He and Elizabeth both loved Scotland and in 1859 he joined her and the girls for a fortnight when they took rooms in an old smuggler's house on the coast at Auchencairn. According to Elizabeth they 'sat and talked and lounged through the hot summer days and the quiet peacefulness of the place was delicious'. William went on from there to the Highlands to shoot, presumably with the Potters, not a pastime in which one would have expected him to participate, but he loved the Highlands, if not the shooting.

In the same year William was asked to become minister at Essex Street, London, one of the most prestigious of pulpits in Unitarian Churches. This was a great honour and evidence of the high regard in which he was held, but he declined. The position was taken by his colleague at Cross Street, James Ham, and a new junior minister James Drummond joined William at Manchester a year later. William had far too many ties binding him to this city that he truly loved and as Elizabeth put it: 'He has made his place here and there must be some stronger reason than an increase in income before it can be right to pull up the roots of a man of his age'. William himself would not have considered his age of fifty-four a reason for declining. He was a fit man who **never shirked hard work. It is certain that he would have** seriously weighed up the alternatives of where he could best serve the cause of Unitarianism and his fellow men and have decided that he should remain in the place where he had sown so many seeds, to nurture them.

His decison to stay was more than justified during the Cotton Famine of 1861-3 when he and Elizabeth were at hand to see the people of Manchester through a time of great hardship. Cotton imports were cut off during the American Civil War and there was mass unemployment in the Lancashire textile trade. The Gaskells helped to organise relief by fund-raising, by distributing food and clothing and setting up training centres where unemployed women were taught sewing. Elizabeth and the older daughters worked long hours at these sewing schools and the whole family were oppressed by the distress around them, 'the one absorbing topic', she described it, 'which was haunting us in our sleep as well as being the first thought on waking and the last at night'. They gave financial as well as practical help and

William readily responded to a request from the Manchester, Sheffield and Lincolnshire Railway Co. to contribute 5 per cent of his dividents to the Distress Relief.

Before the distress reached its peak Cross Street Chapel congregation granted William two months leave of absence in the spring of 1861 and a gift of £50 for a continental holiday, probably an expression of gratitude that he had chosen to remain with them. He went off on his own, at first reluctantly as none of his friends could spend so much time away; but when Elizabeth suggested his staying with William Wetmore Story, an American sculptor and his wife, friends she had made in Rome, 'his face brightened'. He travelled, according to her, in 'a most erratic way through Switzerland and Italy', and on returning to England stayed for a while at Newhaven, not giving any address, as 'he enjoyed being guided by circumstances'.

A further cause for anxiety arose the following year when the Gaskells heard from the Storys that Marianne, who was in Rome for five months with a friend who was wintering there with an invalid son, showed signs of being won over to the Roman Catholic faith. This was a shock particularly to William who, although a tolerant man, was strongly averse to the emphasis on rites and ceremonies in the Catholic Church. It was understandable that Marianne, then twenty-eight, could have temporarily fallen under the spell of the romantic atmosphere in Rome and been influenced by the Catholics she met there, including Cardinal Manning. The whole question was brought out into the open and coolly and sensibly discussed with her parents on her return. She did some serious reading with William, who helped her to reaffirm those Unitarian principles that she had grown up with and possibly had previously accepted unquestioningly.

During these crowded years Elizabeth's attention was frequently diverted from writing and it took her two years to complete her next novel *Sylvia's Lovers* set in Whitby at the time of the Napoleonic Wars. She dedicated it to William with the words 'To my dear husband by her who best knows his value'. It was published in 1863 and she received £1,000 for it and set about planning to spend some of it on further travels for her girls and for William. Before that year was out she had completed yet another short novel that came out in monthly instalments in *Cornhill Mazagine, Cousin Phillis*, a delicate love story no doubt inspired by the sudden engagement and marriage that autumn of Florence, their third daughter, still only twenty, to Charles Crompton, a barrister and son of a judge who lived in style in London. He was thirty and though Flossie was so young and of all the daughters the least confident, and needing the support of her parents, this union met with the approval of William and Elizabeth. They were married by William at Brook Street Chapel in Manchester, in September 1863 and went to live in Hyde Park, London, after a simple wedding for the two families only and a honeymoon such as the Gaskells had enjoyed, in Wales. It was a happy marriage with Charles Crompton proving a kind and tender husband to their precious girl. They saw the young couple frequently as they stayed in Manchester when Charles was on the Northern circuit and William grew very fond of his son-in-law.

Marianne became engaged in 1864 to her second cousin, Edward Thurstan Holland, the son of Elizabeth's cousin, Edwin, so they had known each other from childhood. His parents did not favour the marriage, as they had hoped their eldest son would find a rich wife, being the eldest of eleven children and a brilliant scholar of Eton and Cambridge, and they did not favour the close relationship. William too had reservations, as Marianne was eighteen months older than Thurstan and it would be a long engagement as he had yet to establish himself as a barrister; but William and Elizabeth put no barriers in their way and allowed them to meet freely. Elizabeth confided to her sister-in-law, Anne Robson, that she and William would be able to make the young couple an allowance of £100 a year to help them when they were first married.

Early in 1864, thanks to Elizabeth's contrivance, William had another holiday on the continent. He had been invited by the Storys to stay in Rome during the winter and she was so anxious that he should go that she sought the help of his colleague, John Relly Beard, in obtaining his leave of absence from the Home Missionary Board. She wrote asking him 'to enter into a conspiracy against Mr Gaskell', commenting that he 'will take no steps that can cause the slightest inconvenience to others, least of all to the students'. Elizabeth offered to pay for the services of another teacher to take his place in keeping students up to their work adding 'although probably not so well as Mr Gaskell... You

31. Elizabeth Gaskell in 1864

know how Mr Gaskell will dislike any "fuss"—or asking any favour'. Dr Bear readily agreed and William went off with a clear conscience and returned 'a different creature in consequence', wrote Elizabeth, 'showing the advantage of change and travel'. While he was away in Rome she started on another novel, again to appear in monthly parts in *Cornhill Magazine* for which she was offered an outright payment of £2,000 on completion. This prospect enabled her to give serious thought to a dream she had long cherished, of a home in the country on William's retirement. Surely they deserved, after all these crowded years, to have a chance to relax together in a country home that could be passed on to the unmarried daughters. She would start looking for a house now and then let it until William retired.

Preoccupied as she had been in recent years with the problems of her daughters' adolescence and the delicacy of family relationship, a theme for her novel soon began to take shape in her mind. It would be concerned with the life and loves of two familes living in a country town, once again inspired by her Knutsford girlhood. *Wives and Daughters* was begun and the first instalment appeared in August 1864, and she started on the search for a house, preferably in the south, and enlisted the help of her daughters; but the plan was to be kept a secret from William, once again she was entering into a conspiracy against him, but for his own good.

CHAPTER 9

The Last Years

Throughout their married life Elizabeth had little cause for concern over William's health. He thrived in the Manchester atmosphere where even the spasmodic asthma that he was prone to was unaffected by the smoke. He felt fit and at his best in his own home and did not need to escape from the grimy city as Elizabeth did frequently to raise her spirits. He did not like frosty weather and kept his study well heated, far too warm for Elizabeth, who hated stuffy rooms with closed windows; 'terribly hot' was how she described it when writing to her sister-in-law, Anne Robson, in 1865, 'but that is how he likes it: Sometimes I fancy it is because he cannot regulate the warmth of other houses that he dislikes so much leaving home'. In the same letter she gave a general report on William's health, then in his sixtieth year. 'I wish he was not so thin but that he has been for years now. He has a capital appetite and sleeps like a top at night'. She confided in Anne that occasionally when his liver was out of order he was depressed and easily annoyed 'but in general I would say is much more cheerful and happy in his mind than he used to be when younger'.

His conscientious nature had always made William Gaskell a prey to anxieties concerning others. It is small wonder that the poverty, disease and ignorance that he met with daily, combined with the personal problems of sickness and bereavement that were brought to him by his congregation, troubled his mind, and he was not a man who could easily unburden himself even to so understanding a wife as Elizabeth, but she could read the signs and did her best to relieve him of all petty domestic difficulties.

In 1865 the Cotton Famine was over, the Memorial Hall built and he had an able assistant minister in James Drummond; his daughters were grown women, one happily married and the others still at home. William had every reason to feel easier in his mind and was pursuing his innumerable duties with the vigour and enthusiasm of a much younger man. It was his overworking that Elizabeth feared as she herself was experiencing fatigue, working hard to complete twenty-four pages a month for the new novel that was already appearing in instalments in *Cornhill Magazine*. She pressed on with the work in spite of bouts of

32. The Memorial Hall, Albert Square, Manchester. The meeting place of the Home Missionary Board (see also pages 75-6).

33. James Drummond, assistant minister at Cross Street Chapel 1860-9. From the Chapel photograph album.

prostration, knowing that this novel was going to enable her to buy that house in the country she longed for in readiness for William's retirement. Meta, Julia and Hearn had all been unwell during the year and this made her suspicious of the drains and strengthened her in the decision to move away from Manchester and into the country.

She gave no hint of the plans she had in mind in the long confidential letter to Anne Robson, but a few months later let her American friend, Charles Norton, into the secret. This passage from the letter she wrote to him on 8 September 1865 tells the whole story:

> And then I did a terribly grand thing! and a secret thing too! only you are in America and can't tell. I bought a house and four acres of land in Hampshire - near Alton - for Mr Gaskell to retire to and for a home for my unmarried daughters. That's to say I had not money enough to pay the whole £2,000 but my

publisher advanced the £1,000 on 'an equitable mortgage' and I hope to pay him off by degrees. Mr Gaskell is not to know till then unless his health breaks down before. He is very well and very strong, thank God, but he is sixty and has to work very hard here, his work increasing with his years, and his experience; - in the winter he feels this. The house is large, - (not quite so large as this;) in a very pretty garden (kitchen, flower-garden and paddock between 3 and 4 acres) and in the middle of a pretty rural village; so that it won't be a lonely place for the unmarried daughters who will inherit. In the meantime we are furnishing it (£500 more) and hoping to let it for three years; after which we hope to induce Mr Gaskell to take possession himself. By that time I hope to have paid off the mortgage £1,200 - his two daughters will be most likely married in London; and in London everyone says he will be welcomed as a co-labourer with many of his friends; so that he will not leave off work tho' he will lessen it by the change. 1¾ hrs. will take him to London where his brothers and sister and Florence already are and where we hope Marianne will be by that time. Till then it is a secret from Mr Gaskell. When I have got it *free* we plan many ways of telling him of the pretty home awaiting him.

This was a very big secret for a wife to keep from her husband and the house hunting, purchase and furnishing of The Lawn between June and September had already required a good deal of subterfuge and the telling of white lies. Elizabeth had been aided and abetted throughout by her daughters. She truly believed that William would accept the idea of a removal to a new house on his retirement if it was presented to him as a *fait accompli*, just as he had fallen in with the plans for the holiday in Rome when he had been spared the making of all arrangements. His abhorrence of borrowing money meant that the secret would have to be kept for three years until the mortgage was repaid. During the summer and autumn of 1865 William's suspicions were never aroused. So absorbed was he in his work and so trusting of his wife that he never questioned her absences nor spending of money. Within two months of the writing of the letter to Charles Norton the secret was out in tragic circumstances that no had foreseen.

Elizabeth died suddenly on 12 November. She collapsed and died of a heart attack while taking tea in the drawing room of the house at Alton, in the presence of Meta, Florence, Julia, Charles Crompton and Thurstan Holland. The furnishing was complete, the house let and Elizabeth had come down to see to the final arrangements, leaving Marianne to look after William at Plymouth Grove. She was happy and in high spirits after an exhausting year, rejoicing in the completion of her plans and having written the final chapter of *Wives and Daughters*, all but a few pages but with notes made for the ending. She had driven herself hard throughout the year and was often forced to rest but a heart condition had never been suspected.

The news was brought to William and Marianne by Charles, in person, as all knew that the receiving of the news by telegram would have been a worse shock. William was away from home at Altrincham at a ministers' meeting so word was sent for him to return to Plymouth Grove immediately. This unexpected summons aroused William's suspicions and gravest fears of an impending tragedy so that when the news was broken to him, he had steeled himself to face the worst. The presence of Marianne and Charles sustained him on the sad journey down to Hampshire. His thoughts on seeing The Lawn for the first time must have been conflicting ones: of bitter grief that Elizabeth had stretched herself to the limits to prepare this future home and of wonder at this final demonstration of her love for him and the girls. As was to be expected, Elizabeth's body was brought back to be buried in the grounds of Brook Street Chapel, Knutsford, where the funeral took place on 15 November. William was supported by Thurstan and Charles, his brothers Sam and Robert, and a few close friends. The service was conducted by their old friend Henry Green, minister of the chapel. It was a simple country funeral, such as Elizabeth would have wished.

Cross Street Chapel was crowded on the following Sunday, 19 November, to hear the funeral sermon delivered by James Drummond. He chose as his theme *The Holiness of Human Sorrow*, which he said should be seen not as 'the punishment of man's guilt but the quickener of his nature'. He tried to give William such words of comfort as he had so often himself delivered from the same pulpit to the bereaved. 'It has pleased the Lord to bruise him. He has put him to grief'. he said, and spoke of the suddenness of Elizabeth's death in a way that must have helped those who heard it to accept it with thankfulness for the rounding off of a good life, and concluded with these words: 'In the height of her powers surrounded by a circle bright with the sunshine of her presence and amongst the charm of her conversation she received the mysterious messenger and bowed her head submissive to his call. Her life was joyous to the last and for her such a departure is blessed'.

Ten years previously on the occasion of the death in her forties of Mrs Gallenga, a wife and mother and close friend of Elizabeth's, William had comforted the grieving family with the message that life beyond the grave was in God's hands and all part of a whole life. He chose for the text 'Not my will but Thine be done'.

It was such faith that helped William contain his grief in a way that Thurstan described in a letter he wrote to Charles Norton the day after the funeral, breaking the news. 'Mr Gaskell and the girls are bearing their loss well. He is calm and peaceful and gently resigned to God's will'. Ten years later when writing a letter of condolence to the widow of his friend John Relly Beard, William wrote 'I know from experience what your feelings at present must be... but we do not sorrow as those who are without hope'.

His spirits must have been raised by the general acclaim given to Elizabeth's last novel. The editor of *Cornhill Magazine*, Mr Greenwood, had written some notes to follow the last instalment, to let readers know the ending she had in mind. He concluded the notes with the words 'Here the story is broken off and it can never be finished. What promised to be a crowning work of a life is a memorial of death'. He referred to Elizabeth's gifts as an author and of her books being some of 'the purest works of fiction in the language. And she was herself what her works show her to have been - a wise, good woman'.

Wives and Daughters was generally agreed to be her greatest work and was published in book form, with illustrations by George Du Maurier, in 1866 and ran to several editions in William's lifetime. Sales of Elizabeth's books continued steadily and the income from this source was wisely used and directed into many charitable causes.

William Gaskell never entertained a thought that his pattern of life should be re-designed following his sudden loss. It will always remain a matter of conjecture how he would have taken to a life of retirement in Hampshire. He and the girls never took over The Lawn and he never retired. He remained in Manchester as minister of Cross Street Chapel for another nineteen years, still living at Plymouth Grove with Meta and Julia, who never married.

Marianne and Thurstan were married in 1866 and one of William's rare family letters, written probably after staying with them in Wimbledon, has survived. It gives a clear indication of the happy relationship between him and his daughters. 'It was scribbled in the train at the outset of a journey', wrote Winifred Gerin in her *Life of Elizabeth Gaskell.*

> My dearest Polly,
> I got off very comfortably at 9½, Florence accompanying me to the station and so far I have got *on* very comfortably... and my three fellow passengers like true Englishmen never open their lips or the windows either which is also to my liking. I have begun a similar scribble - under difficulties to Meta. We are now slackening speed for Rugby and I must attack my sandwiches and my brandy and water.
> Leighton Buzzard
> I've finished my sandwiches and brandy and water... and have just been indulging in a bit of your ginger which I found toothsome and pleasant.

The evidence this brief letter gives of the humorous streak in William's nature makes it all the more regrettable that none of his private correspondence survives. What an insight into his character would have been given in the regular letters known to have been exchanged between him and Elizabeth during his absences from home in her lifetime. After 1865 there are no longer any of Elizabeth's letters to her daughters and friends to give us clues to the daily life at Plymouth Grove with comments on William's activities, his health, his moods and his holidays.

There is evidence in plenty of his continuing dedication to his work to be found in minute books and records of the numerous committees on which he served and in the many published sermons and addresses that he gave, for in spite of increasing years he continued to be much in demand as a speaker. His firm faith in the Unitarian beliefs never wavered and was never better expressed that in three splendidly reasoned addresses that he gave when he was nearing his seventies.

One was delivered in Leeds at the bicentenary commemoration service at Mill Hill Chapel, Leeds, on 30 October 1873 when he chose as his subject *The Strong Points of Unitarian Christianity*. This was one of a course of lectures reaffirming Unitarian beliefs in face of criticism by fellow Christians, often due to ignorance. 'We need to stand fair with other Christians', he said, 'and not have our name cast out as evil'. In simple clear language he spelt out his essential beliefs in God as One, not Three in One, in Christ as a real true and noble man and in the Bible as being the only creed; Unitarians reject the principle of original sin and have 'no dread of reason or the light of science', views, he declared, that inspire a more generous confidence in human nature: 'We are created capable of good and it is our duty to promote it'.

In March 1875 he preached to the Manchester District Unitarian Association on *Popular doctrines that obscure the views which the New Testament gives of God*, choosing as his text 'God is Light and in Him there is no darkness at all'. He again appealed to Unitarians to proclaim their beliefs and to strive to make their whole conduct and conversation a recommendation for these beliefs. He concluded: 'Ought we not to feel some concern at the way our Heavenly Father is often made to appear in the light of a hard and cruel tyrant and exert ourselves to display the freeness and fullness and exceeding greatness of His love'?

In May of the same year he addressed an even wider gathering of Unitarians at the 50th annual meeting of the British and Foreign Unitarian Association in Essex Street Chapel in London. This was one of his finest sermons in which he spoke of *The Christianity of Christ*, the text being 'We also believe and therefore speak'. He opened his address with a review of all that had been gained by the Association during its first fifty years through the open declaration of their views that had promoted religious and civil rights for nonconformists, and had won respect for Unitarians, once branded as 'common and unclean'. All who heard him knew how vital a part William Gaskell himself had played in this change of attitude. The second part of his address was an appeal to Unitarians to continue to speak out against the imposition of man-made tenets and ritual. he advocated the Christianity of Christ not the Christianity of the Creed and spelt out Christ's clear message of 'doing justly, loving mercy and walking humbly with God'. At the conclusion of the address he introduced the subject of science which many churchmen considered to be at odds with Christian beliefs, as was later made evident by the controversy over Darwinism. William reaffirmed the Unitarian belief that each new scientific disclosure 'reveals more fully the Creator's glory'.

William's own interest in science was stimulated though membership of Manchester Literary and Philosophical Society during the years when those great architects of modern science,

34. The interior of Cross Street Chapel in 1870. The pulpit stands in front of the organ.

John Dalton and James Joule, were presidents. Here too he met such leading engineers of their day as his friends William Fairbairn and James Nasmyth. He was a member of this Society for forty years and served on its council from 1857 until the end of his life. He took a lively interest in every practical enterprise designed for better living standards and was active in the work of the Manchester and Salford Sanitary Association. This body served as a watchdog over the local authorities after the passing of the Public Health Act in 1848, to ensure that no effort nor money should be spared for the continuing improvement of sanitary conditions. In 1858 the committee of the Association were looking into Manchester Corporation's proposal to charge extra for water used in water closets; in 1867 they brought out a report on public health in Manchester and Salford between 1852 and 1867; in 1875-6 they organised a course of health lectures for the people and in 1877 there was an exhibition of sanitary **appliances in Owens' College grounds**. William found great satisfaction in being concerned in work for the bodily comforts of Manchester's poor and said in a speech in 1878: 'I have always been glad when I could render assistance to objects of practical utility'. Elizabeth had supported him in fund-raising for this association and referred in her letters to helping at the 'Sanitary Bazaars' and also the selling of autographed letters to raise money for this same good cause.

To the committee work that claimed so much of William's time must be added his continuing editorship of the *Unitarian Herald*, published weekly. He shared this work with one of his former students at Manchester New College, the Reverend Brooke Herford. As well as dealing with the literary aspects of editorship, William understood the practical side of the production of the paper and was well up in such matters as costing and printing. One of his few existing letters contains details of the cheapest means of printing posters and advertisements for a lecture that needed publicity.

His lectures on poets, which he had been giving since the early years of his marriage, continued to be popular. The *Manchester Guardian* of 9 March 1872 carried an account of a lecture on 'Crabbe and His Poetry' that he gave to the Eccles Literary and Scientific Society in the Congregational Schoolroom to 'a large and respectable audience;. At the close a vote of thanks was

35. The bust of William Gaskell by G.W. Swynnerton, at the
Portico Library, Manchester. Commissioned by the Library to
mark his thirty years as Chairman in 1878.

passed: with acclamation for his instructive and interesting lecture'.

In one of William's surviving letters to a colleague he listed a
choice of subjects for a lecture which, it appears, he had been
asked to give at short notice. He suggested 'The Poetry of
Common Objects', 'A Few Thoughts on Books and Reading' and
also 'Ballad Poetry' which he said he would prefer but it would
take him longer to prepare.

Close to his heart as scholar and lover of literature must have been the work that he found time to do for the Portico Library, of which he was a member for forty years and its Chairman for thirty. In appreciation of his forty years service in 1878 the proprietors of the Library decided to make him a gift and wrote asking him if he would prefer a bust sculpted by Mr G.W. Swynnerton, or a portrait painted by Miss A. Robinson. William wrote back saying that he thought a portrait would be more desirable, adding: 'My daughters tell me that she has painted a portrait which they like very much (and they are not easily satisfied) but I place myself in the hands of the committee, who are kindly taking some trouble about me, to be "done" as they think best'.

It so happened that enough money was subscribed for both bust and portrait, the bust to be set on a pedestal in the Library and the portrait to be given as a personal present to William. When commissioning the bust the committee stipulated that they did not want their Chairman to be wearing clerical dress, so he was depicted in collar and bow tie with a drapery round his shoulders to match the classical style of Thomas Harrison's bust already displayed in this Library that he designed. Mr Christie when making the presentation made no attempt to conceal the fact that he personally 'was utterly out of harmony with the particular opinions of Unitarians' but William's character rose above religious divisions.

William ended his speech of thanks on a humorous note, saying: 'When towards the end of his life, some great honour was conferred upon Erasmus, he compared it to a pack placed on the back of a sinking horse'. He said that his feelings were very different from Erasmus for he compared this honour now put upon him to 'a warm mash given to an old horse, to enable him to jog on cheerfully for a little while longer'.

William became Principal of the Unitarian Home Missionary Board in 1874 on the retirement of Dr John Relly Beard, a man with whom he had enjoyed a close friendship since their student days at York. That he held Dr Beard in great respect and affection is evident in the form of address he used to his friend in personal letters: *'Vir eruditissimo et amicissimo* and 'My friend, philosopher and guide'. He tried to visit John Beard regularly after his retirement but was frequently too much pressed for time and wrote instead, apologising; on one occasion the reason he gave was the end of term examinations at the College. 'We have been putting

36. The portrait of William Gaskell by Miss Annie Louisa
Robinson (later Mrs Swynnerton) presented by the Portico
Library to the Gaskell family in 1878.

eleven poor fellow creatures to the torture for the greater part of
the day', he wrote, 'I am properly punished with a terrible
headache'.

His work went on too as Visitor and Chairman of the committee of Manchester New College in London until the end of his life. This necessitated frequent visits to London where he could be assured of a warm welcome from the Cromptons and the Thurstan Hollands. He had the added joy of grandchildren, for Marianne became the mother of a baby boy another William, a year after her marriage, and in subsequent years had two other children, Florence, born in 1871, and Bryan, in 1875.

At home he had the constant presence of Meta and Julia, who ran Plymouth Grove as capably as their mother had done. They played a full part in all activities connected with Cross Street Chapel, taught at Mosley Street Sunday School and were involved in numerous charitable works. Like William they were generous with their time and talents and subscribed willingly to many worthy causes. The records of the Domestic Mission among the Cross Street Chapel archives contain regular entries of the donations received from William, Meta and Julia.

At the Chapel William had the backing of two admirable assistant ministers; James Drummond, who had been one of his students at Manchester New College from 1856 to 1859, was at Cross Street Chapel from 1860 until 1869; Samuel Steinthal replaced him and remained in Manchester until after William's death. In common with churches of all denominations in mid to late-Victorian times when church-going was at its peak, Cross Street Chapel had full congregations for its Sunday services, morning, afternoon and evening. William was always in great demand as a preacher at outlying chapels and when unable to go himself he went to pains to find a replacement. 'I have been trying in vain to get somebody to feed the Warrington flock tomorrow', he wrote to a colleague on one occasion. He always made a point of being at Cross Street Chapel on the first Sunday of each month for the Lord's Supper. The number of Unitarian chapels and mission halls in Lancashire and Cheshire had been gradually increasing since the formation of the Provincial Assembly of Presbyterian and Unitarian Ministers in 1820, when just over forty were listed.

William had begun attending meetings of this Assembly in 1822 while still a student at York and his name appears in the minutes of early meetings alongside that of his stepfather, the Reverend Dimock, and he was chosen as preacher in 1824.

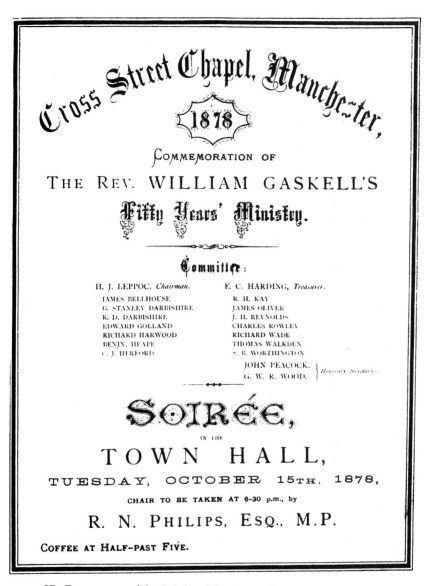

Cross Street Chapel, Manchester,

1878

COMMEMORATION OF

THE REV. WILLIAM GASKELL'S

Fifty Years' Ministry.

Committee:

H. J. LEPPOC, *Chairman.*	E. C. HARDING, *Treasurer.*
JAMES BELLHOUSE	R. H. KAY
G. STANLEY DARBISHIRE	JAMES OLIVER
R. D. DARBISHIRE	J. H. REYNOLDS
EDWARD GOLLAND	CHARLES ROWLEY
RICHARD HARWOOD	RICHARD WADE
BENJN. HEAPE	THOMAS WALKDEN
C. J. HERFORD	S. B. WORTHINGTON

JOHN PEACOCK, }
G. W. R. WOOD, } *Honorary Secretaries.*

SOIRÉE,

IN THE

TOWN HALL,

TUESDAY, OCTOBER 15TH, 1878,

CHAIR TO BE TAKEN AT 6-30 p.m., by

R. N. PHILIPS, ESQ., M.P.

COFFEE AT HALF-PAST FIVE.

37. Programme of the Soirée celebrating William Gaskell's fifty years ministry at Cross Street Chapel, 1878.

William went on to become President of the Assembly from 1865 onwards. The Provincial Assembly was connected to the British and Foreign Unitarian Association to whom he gave his address on *The Christianity of Christ*. In 1872 the Provincial Assembly presented him with a portrait of himself painted by Mr W. Percy, to mark his fiftieth year of membership. It was placed in the large room of the Memorial Hall. It hangs today in the Unitarian College, Victoria Park (see frontispiece).

The fiftieth anniversary of William Gaskell's ministry at Cross Street Chapel was marked by a great demonstration of affection and appreciation for his work as preacher, teacher and public-spirited citizen of Manchester A soirée was held in Manchester Town Hall on 15 October 1878 at which over 1,000 people attended to see the presentation of gifts and to hear the speeches. After tea and coffee had been served in the sculpture gallery all moved to the large hall for the ceremony. Some months previously a commemoration fund had been opened to which his congregation and friends had subscribed. At William's request £1,750 of the money raised was to be used to found a Gaskell Scholarship to Owens' College, for third year students of the Unitarian Home Missionary Board. It was to be awarded on the result of an examination in Greek, Latin, maths and an English essay. On display in the Town Hall was the personal gift to William from the Cross Street Chapel congregation of a set of plate that comprised an inscribed solid silver centre piece, four compotiéres burnished with gold, a pair of antique vases, a gilt jug and two goblets. The presentation was made after the platform party had been greeted by cheering and the singing of 'Auld Lang Syne'. Speeches followed from the many bodies for whom William had worked and tributes were showered upon him, perhaps best summed up in the words of the Reverend George Henry Wells speaking for the Provincial Assembly who ended thus: 'Your high character and your richly-cultivated mind have given you an influence far beyond the limits of our own religious communion'.

William was obviously moved by the speeches as he admitted in his reply: 'As you must have seen I have been too much overcome by them to acknowledge the tributes adequately'. He said that he valued the testimonials as highly as the beautiful gifts 'as a manifestation of regard from such a large number of friends'. He found room too for a little touch of humour and when commenting on a request he had recently received to preach a Sunday School sermon again next year, in view of the heavy collection on the previous occasion, said 'This may be taken as some little proof that there is still a little work left in me'. The evening ended with the singing of the anthem 'Let everyone that hath breath praise the Lord, Hallelujah'.

A commemorative service had been held at Cross Street Chapel the previous August when William had preached the sermon on the text 'Ask now of the days that are past' and reviewed the changes he had seen in attitudes towards Unitarianism, concluding 'My heart's desire has been to work with you and for you to the best of my ability'.

And he did serve them for another six years. He still took regular holidays with his friends, the Potters, and a delightful glimpse of him in a relaxed mood when on holiday with them at Dalguise is given in her journal by Beatrix Potter, the granddaughter of his old friend Edmund. She recorded this memory of him in her private journal. 'He is sitting comfortably in the warm sunshine on the doorstep at Dalguise in his grey coat and old felt hat. The newspaper lies on his knee, suddenly he looks up with his gentle smile. There are sounds of pounding footsteps. The bluebottles whizz off the path. A little girl in a pink frock and striped stockings bounds to his side and offers him a bunch of meadowsweet. He just says "thank you" and puts his arm round her'. Beatrix was the little girl and a photograph of this charming scene was taken by her father, Rupert, who was a professional photographer. When Beatrix was eight she knitted Mr Gaskell a comforter and sent it to him for his birthday. He wrote back thanking her: 'Big as I am I know I could not have done it one-tenth as well. Every time I put it round my neck, which during the winter will be every day, I shall be sure to think of you'.

Little Beatrix may have reminded William of the happy days of his own daughters' childhood when he went snowballing and flying kites with them. These memories must have been particularly poignant when Flossie died in 1881 at the early age of thirty-nine. Beatrix Potter recorded in her journal in 1882 that Mr Gaskell was due to arrive on 8 August to stay with them at Wray Castle on Lake Windermere where they were spending several

38. William Gaskell with Beatrix Potter, as a girl, from a
photograph taken in the late 1870s by her father, Rupert
Potter.

months. The next time his name appears in the journal is on 3 April 1884, when she was staying in Manchester. 'Went to see Mr Gaskell. He will not last long I'm afraid'. He lasted only another six weeks. On 12 June when she was with her parents in Oxford she recorded: 'Papa heard from Mr Steinthal that Mr Gaskell died at five yesterday morning. Dear old man, he has had a very peaceful end. If ever anyone led a blameless peaceful life it was he. There has always been a deep childlike affection between him and me'. On 14 June she wrote: 'Four o'clock Saturday afternoon. Mr Gaskell is just being buried beside his wife. We have sent some flowers'.

William's health began to fail that year. He was now seventy-eight but had been well enough to attend the committee meeting and Annual General Meeting of the Portico Library on 3 and 4 January when he was once again appointed Chairman and his name headed the list in a ballot for the appointment of trustees. He became aware of his age and increasing weariness after preaching at Cross Street on 13 January. This proved to be his last sermon. He felt he could no longer give of his best and relinquished all his duties. The next six months he spent at home and slowly faded away being taken seriously ill with bronchitis only a few days before his death. The funeral service and burial took place at Brook Street Chapel, Knutsford, and was private, but a large number of friends came from Manchester and ministers from surrounding areas to pay their respects. Alfred Steinthal took the service and called upon all present to thank God that William Gaskell's own wish had been granted that up to the last he should be 'about his Father's business'.

The following day Mr Steinthal preached the memorial sermon in Cross Street Chapel, this time taking as his text 'If you have loved me you would have rejoiced because I go to the Father', appropriately chosen for a man whom the preacher said had led 'a complete and consistent life'. How hard he must have found it to find new words in which to express the high regard in which William had been held.

No more fitting words can be found to end the account of the life and death of William Gaskell than his own 'Burial Song for a Good Man'.

Calmly, calmly lay him down!
He hath fought the noble fight
He hath battled for the right;
He hath won the unfading crown.

All that makes for human good,
Freedom, righteousness and truth,
Objects of aspiring youth
Firm to age he still pursued.

Memories all too bright for tears
Crown around us from the past;
Faithful toiled he to the last, -
Faithful through unflagging years.

Kind and gentle was his soul
Yet it glowed with glorious might;
Filling clouded minds with light
Making wounded spirits whole.

Hoping, trusting, lay him down!
Many in the realms of love
Look for him with eyes of love
Wreathing his immortal crown.

39. The Gaskell family grave at Brook Street Chapel, Knutsford.

CHAPTER 10

A Century on

A century after William Gaskell's death his former home is still a meeting place where newcomers to Manchester can find a warm welcome. The house at Plymouth Grove, now numbered 84, has been put to a purpose that he and Elizabeth could never have envisaged and one that would have delighted them. Since 1970 it has been the headquarters of the International Society, run by Manchester University as a meeting place for overseas students, their friends and relatives, and provides residential accommodation for a small number. The room that was William's study still retains its bookshelves and wooden shutters and is the reading room. The spacious drawing room and dining room are common rooms for members and the former schoolroom is converted into an office, where preserved in a corner is a small pane of glass on which are scratched the names of Florence and Julia, with the date 1855, when they were children of thirteen and nine.

The unmarried daughters, Meta and Julia, who continued to live in the house after their father's death left their mark on the house in other less superficial ways, following their parents' example of offering warm and generous hospitality within their home. They were always busy, giving generously of their time and money to philanthropic, educational and social schemes, serving on numerous committees. Thanks to the steady income that accrued through royalties on the sales of their mother's books they were able to give financial support to causes in which they were particularly concerned, the care of the sick and needy and the nursing and teaching professions, the work of Cross Street Chapel, the Domestic Mission, the Unitarian College, Manchester College, Oxford, and the Portico Library.

Both were Liberals but did not take an active part in politics and were not sympathetic towards the suffragettes, considering that women's welfare came before women's rights. They both took a keen interest in higher education for women and served as governors on the board of Manchester High School for Girls. They were founders of Manchester Social Club, an offspring of the Lower Mosley Street Schools, where they had once taught with their mother at the Sunday School, and now realised the need for young men and women working in Manchester to have a place to meet under pleasant conditions. In addition the Misses Gaskell bought a piece of land opposite their home and it became the Gaskell Recreation Ground.

Their own social life was conducted in the same un-ostentatious manner as during William's and Elizabeth's lifetime; visitors were assured of a sympathetic hearing and lively conversation from these two women who had in early girlhood associated with many of Manchester's leading citizens and their mother's literary contemporaries. After Mrs Gaskell's death they took on her role of hostess to the many men and women of wide-ranging interests who came to see William: throughout their lifetime Meta and Julia retained a keen appreciation of the arts, treasuring the beautiful family possessions of pictures, china and furniture that their parents had gradually added to their home. When tram-lines were laid along Plymouth Grove they campaigned vigorously for the preservation of the trees that lined the road.

Like their mother Meta and Julia were always glad to escape from Manchester to the peace of Silverdale, and went abroad regularly to the Swiss Alps; they inherited their father's love of hill-walking and were keen mountaineers and were the first women to negotiate one of the Swiss mountain passes. They built a cottage at Silverdale which they named The Sheiling, not far from Lindeth Tower, with a view over the sea and fells. It is still a private house and at one period was occupied by the poet and playwright, Gordon Bottomley and his wife, who were visited there by the poet Edward Thomas, who described it in a letter to Eleanor Farjeon as 'a really lovely house in position - on a stoney hill all alone with rabbits on the doorstep'. This was in June 1914 and the house made such an impression that he was inspired to write this poem:

The Sheiling

It stands alone
Up in a land of stone
All worn like ancient stairs,
A land of rocks and trees
Nourished on wind and stone.

And all within
Long delicate has been;
By arts and kindliness
Coloured, sweetened and warmed
For many years has been.

Safe resting there
Men hear in the travelling air
But music, pictures see
In the same daily land
Painted by the wild air.

One maker's mind
Made both, and the house is kind
To the land that gave it peace,
And the stone has taken the house
To its cold heart and is kind.

Lindeth Tower is still standing and so is Lindeth Lodge that the Gaskells always spoke of as Wolf House; this is now the Wolf House Gallery of Arts and Crafts and retains is wolf crest.

Meta and Julia were inseparable companions and when Julia died suddenly on 26 October 1908 at the age of sixty-two Meta was heartbroken and her health deteriorated. Flags on Manchester Town Hall were flown at half mast on the day of Julia's funeral which took place at the old chapel at Knutsford. Meta bought two adjoining houses in Plymouth Grove and had them converted into a nursing home as a memorial to Julia and concerned herself in its management until she became too disabled by bodily pain to continue. She died on 27 October 1913 and at her own request there were no flowers or music at the funeral that took place at Knutsford, where a detachment of nurses lined the path to the chapel. Her name was added to Julia's and her parents' at the base of the simple marble cross that surmounts the family grave, a place much visited by lovers of Mrs Gaskell's books on their pilgrimage to her 'Cranford'. The Lawn at Alton that Mrs Gaskell visualised as a home for William's old age and for the unmarried daughters was never occupied by any of the Gaskells. It is now an Old People's Home and so is put to a use which would have pleased the family.

Although playing so important a part in public life both the Miss Gaskells shunned personal publicity and were never eager to disclose personal family details to those anxious for biographical information concerning their mother; they are known to have destroyed many family letters.

When Marianne died in 1920 she was buried beside her husband in Alfrick churchyard, Worcestershire, where they had lived at The Court. Edward Thurstan Holland had died in the same year as William Gaskell, at the age of forty-eight. There was one grandchild, Margaret, the daughter of William Holland and his wife Florence. Margaret married Clifford Trevor Jones and bore him a daughter, Elizabeth, who became Mrs Jack Dabbs. Their children, Timothy William, born in 1954, and Sarah Jane, born in 1958, are in the direct line of descent from William and Elizabeth and are their great-great-great grandchildren.

In her will Meta Gaskell left many generous bequests to the numerous organisations in which she and Julia had been involved, including £1,000 and her father's fiftieth anniversary gift of gold plate, to Manchester University. The estate was valued at £50,223 and when the house and contents were sold many hoped that Manchester City Council would purchase the property and maintain it as a Gaskell museum; but it was bought by a private purchaser and remained a residence until it became the property of Manchester University in 1970. An energetic campaign was fought by those who had the vision to see a way in which this historic property could be put to an appropriate use as the headquarters of the International Society founded in 1966. This Society operates as a welfare and information centre for the many overseas students who come to study in the Greater Manchester area at universities, polytechnics, colleges and hospitals. One of its stated aims is 'to try and ensure that new students arriving in Manchester from overseas are given a warm welcome in a part of the country noted for its friendliness'. William Gaskell would have marvelled to see the growth of Owens' College from small beginnings to the huge University of today and the great spread of buildings, at the very centre of which his home has been preserved to play its part in promoting true brotherhood.

The building that was as close to his heart as his home has undergone a transformation, but only in outward appearance. This is Cross Street Chapel, that suffered devastating damage in the wartime blitz on Manchester in December 1940. Mr Harry Hewerdine, for many years chairman of the Chapel committee and keenly interested in the Chapel's history, gives this account of the damage to the building and the way in which the people of Cross Street Chapel were undaunted by the tragedy. He writes:

Only the four walls of the 1694 building were left standing, the interior was completely gutted but the two main doors were intact and also most of the leaded windows. Fortunately the schoolhouse, and the historic Chapel Room, that was built on to the Chapel in 1734, was unscathed and services continued without interruption on the following Sunday. Services were occasionally held on the bombed site in the open air. An extra large army hut was obtained through the generosity of two chapel members who belonged to the Adelphi Lads' Club and this was erected in the centre of the Chapel site enclosure, serving for many years as a city church, and over the inside doorway were these words of welcome: 'Let no man be a stranger here'. When the new Chapel building was commenced in 1958 the hut was given to Urmston Unitarian Church and has been in constant use ever since.

The Cross Street congregation made a public appeal for a modest £10,000. Payment of £20,000 was received from the War Damage Commissioners and the remainder was met by the generosity of members and from Chapel funds. The new building designed by the architects Messrs. Halliday and Agate was opened on 21 March 1959 by the president of the General Assembly of Unitarian and Free Christian Churches, the Rt. Hon. Chuter Ede MP.

A symbolic figure entitled 'Rebirth' and fashioned out of a charred beam rescued from the old building now stands in the Chapel. Many of the church memorials were shattered in the blitz but the tablet in memory of Elizabeth Gaskell was rescued and is placed just inside the main doorway. William Gaskell's memorial tablet was beyond recovery so no one today can read this moving tribute to Cross Street Chapel's longest serving minister.

Sacred to the memory of
The Reverend William Gaskell M.A.
Who died on the 11th of June 1884 in his 79th year
His remains lie at Knutsford with those of his dear wife.
A scholar of wide culture and refined taste,
a master of English speech,
an able teacher of
young women and young men in many different circles,
a consistent Liberal in politics and religion,
he lived a busy life of influence and honour
and died greatly regretted by his fellow citizens.

In this place
He will ever be remembered
for his faithful ministry
in which he fulfilled by his example
as well as in his preaching and his pastorate,
a very lovely ideal of Christian piety and duty.
This memorial of their affection
is erected by his mourning congregation.

An innovation to Cross Street Chapel since William Gaskell's day that is a familiar sight to all passers-by today is the notice board outside the chapel carrying its 'Thought for the Week' and known as the Wayside Pulpit. Cross Street Chapel was the first place of worship in Great Britain to use this method of spreading the word that is now a common sight outside churches and chapels. From the beginning the Cross Street Chapel messages were short and pithy, and chosen to appeal to 'the man in the street rather than the man in the pew', as Mr A. Vincent Wilson phrased it in his *A short history of Cross Street Chapel's Wayside Pulpit*, written to mark the fiftieth anniversary. 'The Thought for the Week' has appeared with absolute regularity since 26 December 1920, handprinted by a member of the Chapel, and this is how it has continued, a new message appearing every week, often chosen for its appropriateness to the season or to

40. The interior of the new Cross Street Chapel, designed by
Halliday and Agate, 1959.

national or local events or to the subject of the current course of
sermons. Sentimental and strongly evangelical messages are
avoided and the Cross Street Chapel selection ranges over a wide
field of conventional wisdom, literary allusion and philosophical
reflection that cause the passer-by to pause and think. Many
letters have been received by ministers of the Chapel from
people saying how much they have been helped by the words
they have read. Since 1921 each year's messages have been
printed in a small booklet at Christmas time and serves as an
ideal form of Christmas greeting. The first message of each year
is supplied by the Lord Mayor and this link with the civic
authority is greatly valued.

Examples of messages used in 1982 were: 'The size of a person's world is the size of his heart'. 'We never get a second
chance to make a good first impression'. 'There are tones of voice

that mean more than words. 'Strangers are friends we haven't met'.

In his foreword, today's minister, the Reverend E.J. Raymond Cook, writes: 'Cross Street Messages challenge us to think for ourselves... he would be a fastidious reader who in the course of a year found nothing to make him think about the human condition or did not move him to do the little that in him lies to atone for "Man's inhumanity to man"'.

William Gaskell, lover of English literature, would have fully supported the idea of the Wayside Pulpit and would also have contributed to the monthly publication, the *Chapel Calendar*, which conveys a strong sense of a united community. The following heading at the top of every page of this magazine gives a simple definition of the Chapel's constitution; 'The affairs of the Chapel are governed by the decision of the general meeting of members of the congregation. There are normally two meetings of the members, the Annual General Meeting in the spring and the half-yearly meeting in the autumn. No doctrinal test of any kind is imposed upon the minister, members or others who attend the service'.

In spite of the fact that this church is in the centre of the city, surrounded by offices and shops, the community spirit of a closely knit suburban or village church is apparent at Cross Street. There are two services on Sundays, morning and evening, and a lunchtime service each Wednesday when a lunch is served and anyone may drop in; many city workers attend this service and congregations are often larger than on a Sunday, so 'strangers become friends' as the Wayside Pulpit suggests. There is an active Women's League, organising fund-raising and social and devotional meetings, and a smaller Men's League. The Domestic Mission is still in existence and to mark its one hundred and fiftieth anniversary the Manchester District Association presented a cheque for £500, as Trustee of the Domestic Mission Fund, to the Lord Mayor of Manchester's Charity, earmarked for the Salvation Army's Crossley House in Ancoats. These Homes care for elderly people who have in many cases lived in destitution and are without family. The cheque was presented in the presence of a representative gathering at a reception held in Cross Street Chapel. Rooms at the Chapel are let to outside organisations, so there is much coming and going to and from the Chapel. Pedestrianisation of nearby streets has made Cross Street a very busy thoroughfare but the Chapel remains a quiet and secure retreat from the turmoil of the twentieth century.

Another building and meeting place frequently visited by William for nearly forty years and closely associated with the Chapel, was destroyed by fire in the blitz. This was the house at 36, George Street which had been the home of the Manchester Literary and Philosophical Society since 1799. The Society had previously met at Cross Street Chapel. Many valuable and historic contents including apparatus, furniture, paintings and documents were lost in the fire and can never be replaced, but a new building was erected on an enlarged site in 1960. Unfortunately structural defects appeared in the building after twenty years, too costly to remedy, so it was sold and the Society took over office accommodation for its headquarters and held its meetings at different venues. Since 1981 when the 'Lit. and Phil.' celebrated its bicentenary, occasional meetings have been held again at Cross Street Chapel where the Society had its beginnings with a membership of 25, now risen to over 700.

The Portico Library where William was Chairman for thirty years escaped with only superficial damage from the bombing but there have been some changes to the fine old building since his day. He would have used the dignified porticoed entrance on Mosley Street to the Library but today's members go in by the side door climbing the back stairway to the upper floor. The ground floor was for many years let to a bank that was housed in the hollow well, encircled by the galleried first floor whose walls are still lined with bookcases and lit by the central dome of Thomas Harrison's design that was such an important feature of the building.The ground floor, once the newsroom, with newspaper stands, reference books and a globe of the world, is now sealed off from the upstairs gallery by a modern ceiling and small glazed dome. The members' room leading off from the upstairs gallery is unchanged and William's bust stands beside the table where he once presided at the committee meetings. The room is still comfortably furnished with armchairs where members can recline to read and enjoy light refreshments and retains a club atmosphere. There are between 30,000 and 40,000 volumes in the Library acquired since its opening in 1806, among them many first editions of books on travel, local history and architecture. The Library still prides itself on supplying the latest books requested by individual members and follows the first rule printed in the catalogue of 1810: 'A book shall be on the table in the Reading Room for subscribers to enter their recommendations of books'. The old minute books contain records of the purchase of books agreed upon by the committee with William Gaskell's signature appended. Among the last approved purchases to which he put his signature in January 1884 were *The Story of Chinese Gordon* and *Rhymes and Reason* by Lewis Carroll. Women were admitted as members just before the First World War and now comprise about a quarter of today's membership of 200. It is one of the last six remaining public subscription libraries. Art exhibitions open to the public are held regularly at the Portico, the pictures being displayed round the gallery against the inner dome.

In 1983 one of the Portico's rare possessions and a link with

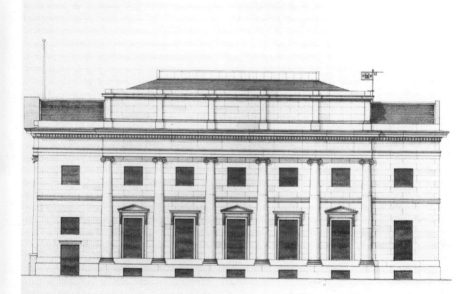

41. The Portico Library, Manchester, Charlotte Street elevation, 1983, from a drawing by A.J. Pass. The new wind vane can be seen above the roof on the right.

John Dalton, which had been out of use since late Victorian times, was restored to working order. This is a wind dial with a new stainless steel vane; it is hoped it will serve to publicise the efforts the Library is making to raise funds to restore the building to its former glory. John Dalton was granted free membership of the Portico in return for seeing to the wind dial and the Library clock, which has also been restored. Mr Norman Harvey of the Antiquarian Horological Society is responsible for this work and has been appointed 'John Dalton member in charge of clocks'.

Fire bombs only did light damage to the roof of the Memorial Hall, the building that William Gaskell had seen erected for the use of the Unitarian Home Missionary Board as a lecture hall; but the Hall had not been used by the Board since 1905 when, renamed the Unitarian Home Missionary College, it moved to residential premises in Victoria Park. The building still stands today in Albert Square, the carved lettering over the doorway reminding passers-by of its origins. When the Hall was no longer required by the Unitarian College a board of trustees was formed to manage the property which was let off floor by floor to various tenants including the Manchester Photographic Society and the Kardomah Café. An understanding was reached with the tenants that the Unitarians could have the use of a room there once a year. The building was sold in 1972 and there was talk of its being demolished, but fortunately, thanks to a campaign led by Unitarians, a Preservation Notice was put on it.

The Unitarian Home Missionary College, now retitled the Unitarian College, still has the same premises in Victoria Park for the training of Unitarian ministers and is affiliated to the Manchester University Faculty of Theology. It runs an Arts Degree Course followed by a Theological Course of five or six years and a two or three year part-time course for General Assembly students training as lay pastors. As in William Gaskell's day at the Home Missionary Board, students have practical experience in preaching at churches in the region. Since 1927 the College has been a University hall of Residence and has accommodation for thirty students. In the 1982-3 session six students were training for the ministry, including two women. The College is inevitably feeling the effect of inflation but the Principal, the Reverend J. Arthur Long in the 128th Annual Report wrote with hope: 'So

42. Unitarian College, Victoria Park, Manchester.

long as we have students for the ministry - and at the moment considering the many adverse factors which exist, our prospects remain remarkably good - we are sure the U.C.M. will remain in business, somehow or another'.

Unitarian ministers are still being trained today at Manchester College, Oxford, where there is accommodation for seventy students, some of them taking courses in English literature, social studies, music, philosophy and history as well as theology and religion. William Gaskell never lived to see the removal of his old college, formerly Manchester New College, from London to Oxford. Perhaps he would initially have disapproved of the move, as Dr Martineau did, fearing that at Oxford the College would be isolated from nonconformist influences. At the time of the removal to London, William had advocated the College's return to Manchester for the same reason but once the decision was made he had worked as earnestly as ever for the College, journeying regularly to London as Chairman of the committee and Visitor. It was a brave action to establish a new theological school at Oxford in 1889 at a time when funds were low and student numbers short. The first Principal at Oxford was James Drummond who had been with William Gaskell at Cross Street

43. The Chapel, Manchester College, Oxford, designed by
Thomas Worthington, himself a Unitarian.

Chapel from 1860 to 1869. Under his guidance and that of his
successors the great principles of freedom of thought and high
scholarship have been maintained at Oxford and as the prospec-
tus for 1983-4 declares its purpose is still 'to impart theological
instruction in an atmosphere of intellectual freedom'.

Manchester University has grown beyond recognition from
the first Owens' College in Quay street that William Gaskell
knew. University buildings now engulf the part of the city where
he lived and worked and the development of the University of
Manchester Institute of Science and Technology would have
appealed to William Gaskell who took a keen interest in scientific
and technological advances. He would have rejoiced to see the
clearing of slum areas and the rising of these new seats of learning where young men and women have opportunities to gain
knowledge in so many fields and equip themselves for life.

One college of education, not associated with the University
and attended by men and women of all ages, would have given
him particular pleasure as it is a direct descendant of the old
Mosley Street Day and Sunday Schools started by Unitarians
where he and his wife and daughters taught. Evidence of this
link can be seen in the entrance hall of today's College of Adult

Education in All Saints where a memorial tablet is placed that recalls John Ogle Curtis, appointed headmaster of the schools in 1836 by the committee on which John Robberds and William Gaskell sat. This tablet, first placed in the Mosley Street bulding on the death of John Curtis, pays tribute to the man 'who during 22 years laboured with conscientious fidelity and unwearying patience of love... and by his wise instruction and Christian example left lasting influences on the hearts and lives of many for good'. When the building was demolished in 1896 to make way for the Midland Hotel, the railway company built new premises for the schools on a site near Central Station. It remained there continuing its work through the changing times that followed the dawn of the twentieth century, but after the First World War its educational function was superseded by social activities and it became the Manchester Social Club which the Misses Gaskell supported. After the Second War it was reborn as the College of Adult Education under Manchester Education Committee with Mr Lester Burney as Warden. He tells the story of the development of the college from the early schools in his book *Cross Street Chapel Schools* and his plan to make this 'a college in the city where men and women between the ages of eighteen and eighty could find something in a wide range of interests to suit their age, ability and aptitude and to pursue these interests in a friendly homely atmosphere'. In the same way as working men thirsty for knowledge flocked to William Gaskell's lectures on poetry and English literature so did men and women after the grim years of war seize the opportunity to catch up on their education that had been cut short, eager to put their new-found leisure to good purpose.

After over thirty years on this site the College was on the move again as planners and developers were appropriating every available space in the city. A fine new building was built at All Saints that fulfils the two requirements of the College that were Mr Burney's aim, providing every facility for learning in a friendly atmosphere. The present building has well-lit class-rooms, lecture halls, meeting rooms, space for exhibitions, music room, theatre and canteen and the spirit of the social club of former times pervades the place. A permanent reminder of the Mosley Street Schools where men, women and children found the same refreshment and uplift to the spirits in humbler surroundings, can be found on the site where the second building stood, on the arches above some of the ground floor windows in the Midland Hotel, which are decorated with terracotta figures representing Literature, Science and the Arts.

It is however in more vital ways than by stone figures and memorial tablets that the influence of William Gaskell and his contemporaries is still felt today in Manchester and beyond. As a preacher he spread the Word from Cross Street Chapel pulpit for over fifty years and in so doing rooted the old Chapel still more firmly in the hearts of Manchester people. Though other city churches and chapels were emptied as Manchester citizens moved out to the suburbs as transport improved, Cross Street Chapel endures despite the blitz, and the Truth is still being declared from there today, even if for many it is only read, in passing, on the Wayside notice board.

As husband and father William Gaskell knit his family together and with Elizabeth made their home at Plymouth Grove a centre of philanthropy, friendship and creativity and so it continues today and, though in a new guise, it is still a home.

As a lover of English literature he imbued others with a love of the language, several of the hymns he wrote are still sung today, and books still crowd the shelves of the library he served. As a teacher he brought light into dark places beginning with a simple Sunday School in a humble building and continuing until there were no barriers to university education and working men could train for the ministry. There are still over fifty Unitarian Churches in the north-west, the same number as in the eighteen-eighties. His own old college will be celebrating its bicentenary in 1986, two hundred years after the founding of the first Manchester Academy.

William Gaskell's firm religious faith carried him through a long and crowded life of service to others and gave to all who met him an insight into the life-affirming Unitarian beliefs in the goodness and value of individual human beings. There is a place in today's confused world for a re-assessment of a sense of values and a return to such clear and simple standards for living as William set himself. Unitarians helped to steer men and women through the upheavals of the Industrial Revolution; perhaps they have a still more important part to play in dispelling the doubts and fears of the Nuclear Age.

Appendices

Cross Street Chapel in the twentieth century

On the face of it there could be no greater contrast than that between the nineteenth century and the twentieth: between church-going Victorian society in which Spurgeon's Tabernacle was a 'must' for the provincial visitor to London and the 'secular society' of to-day: yet to put the differences between them in these terms is to over-simplify. Beneath the surface calm of the Victorian Age seethed the miseries of the masses who had no share in its prosperity, hardships, deprivations and the resultant indifference to organised religion revealed in the Reports of the Ministry to the Poor inaugurated at Cross Street Chapel in 1833. The people of Cross Street did what they could to alleviate suffering by their philanthropic endeavours though they did not envisage any radical change in the class structure of society - that was left to Marx and Engels - but they insisted that the crumbs which fell from the rich man's table should be both more generous and more nutritious. A number of them enlightened employers of labour themselves, they reminded those who were not, of their duty to those whose labour had made them rich. To acknowledge the limitations of Victorian philanthropy is in no wise to diminish it.

The mid-century saw the emergence of tensions of another kind generated by scientific discovery, especially in geology and biology, which affected all the deeper minds of the time. It now appeared that, far from having been created in the 'six days' of the Book of Genesis, the ancestry of Man stretched far beyond into 'the dark backward and abysm of time'. The Record of the

Rocks was set against the Record of the Book. Reactions to the new knowledge varied. Some, like Philip Gosse, himself a naturalist of repute, clung to Genesis as might have been expected from a man who denied his small son Edmund Christmas pudding because it was 'meat offered to idols'! The conflict between religion and science was waged with bigotry and bitterness and lingers on to-day notwithstanding that it rests on a 'category mistake'. What was at issue then as now was the authority of the Bible but a Bible mis-read as a text-book of science. Through all the 'great debate', not even now consigned to the realm of 'old, far off, forgotten things and battles long ago', the nature of the free religious faith of the Unitarians secured them against the conflicts which divided others. They did not have to choose between blind bibliolatry and total scepticism because for them the 'Seat of Authority' was the soul of Man enlightened by the Divine Spirit. On the one hand they welcomed new knowledge, while on the other they saw with Kierkegaard that 'When everything is explained by an 'x' which is not itself explained, nothing is explained', a dictum worthy of remembrance in an age like ours when for many people science has all the answers.

It is not, however, in scientific discovery or in religious controversy that the decisive difference between the nineteenth century and the twentieth is to be found but in the two World Wars which changed the face of England, of Europe and of the world. In both there were rumours of the impending closure of Cross Street Chapel. In 1917 its then minister, Revd. E.L.H. Thomas, rebutted them in *Illustrations of Cross Street Chapel,* a unique photographic record of Chapel treasures, some of them since lost for ever. The fate of the Old Chapel in the Second World War was no easily exposed rumour but part of a still greater tragedy, a holocaust which set Manchester and Salford literally on fire and killed a thousand of their people in one night. Nothing could ever be the same after that! Of Henry Newcome's Chapel, opened in 1694 and virtually unchanged since then, only the walls were left standing, yet miraculously under a succession of able ministers continuity was maintained unbroken and those who cried 'Ichabod! Ichabod! the glory has departed' were to be proved wrong.

Mr Thomas was followed as minister by Revd. H.H. Johnson,

a scholar deeply versed in French and German literature and a powerful preacher who filled the Chapel to capacity. One of his innovations was the discussion hour following his evening sermon at a time, 1919, when the First World Was had left many people doubting the justice of God and despairing of Man; but the one which brough him national publicity was his Wayside Pulpit Messages, the first of which, 'Don't Worry, It May Never Happen', was reproduced in a great variety of media. The idea of the Wayside Pulpit had come from America but this was the first to appear in England. For many years the Messages were hand-printed by Mr Vincent Wilson, a man of many talents who is still active in spite of infirmities at ninety-two. The Messages have appeared every week without a break ever since, even, almost unbelievably, the day after the blitz of Christmas, 1940.

The ministerial succession was also maintained without lengthy intermissions. Revd. C.W. Townsend who followed Harrold Johnson is remembered alike for his bracing personality and his robust preaching. Revd. F.H. Amphlett Micklewright who succeeded him was a man of formidable erudition and brilliant oratorical gifts whose involvement in the public life and political affairs of the city made him a controversial figure. After a meteoric ministry at Cross Street he returned to the Anglican Church from whence he had come. His learning was manifest in his book *The Religion of To-morrow*. Mr Micklewright is an authority on Canon Law in which he holds a Doctorate. Revd. Fred Kenworthy who followed him in the Cross Street pulpit was a gentleman of a very different stamp who impressed people by his quiet demeanour; but he, too, was a scholar, a lecturer at the University of Manchester and subsequently Principal of the Unitarian College in Victoria Park. His untimely death very soon after his retirement from that office was a loss to the Unitarian movement. His successor was Revd. Dr Reginald W. Wilde. A practising psychotherapist as well as a faithful pastor, Dr Wilde contributed to the literature of psychology books conspicuous for their sanity, balance and freedom from the extremism of some schools of thought. A manual of devotions he compiled from a great diversity of sources is still freely drawn upon in Cross Street services. The outstanding event of Dr Wilde's ministry was the opening of the new Chapel in 1959. It was he who organised the preparations for it, only to die a few weeks before it took place. It was supremely fitting that the new pulpit should be dedicated to Henry Newcome and Reginald Wilde, joined as they were and made contemporaries by a bond of the Spirit spanning and transcending well-nigh three centuries of history. In them 'The successiveness of Man was embraced by the simultaneity of God'.

Revd. Charles H. Bartlett who followed Dr Wilde was also a psychotherapist. To his guidance some members of the Chapel itself as well as a wider constituency of other patients have borne witness by a successful re-adjustment of their lives. Mr Bartlett was also an accomplished musician who recognised the therapeutic value of music. He was a man of great generosity which was sometimes exploited. He also made substantial contributions to Unitarian literature. His life, too, was prematurely cut off at the height of his powers. It is melancholy to reflect that whereas four eighteenth - and nineteenth - century ministries totalled some two hundred years between them, the mortality rate among twentieth - century incumbents has been abnormally high.

E.J. Raymond Cook
Minister of Cross Street Chapel
Manchester

Manchester District Association of Unitarian and Free Churches

I am indebted to Mr Geoffrey Head, Honorary General Secretary of the Manchester District Association of Unitarian Churches, for the following account of William Gaskell's services to the Association from its foundation in 1859 until his death in 1884.

William Gaskell was the President/Chairman of the M.D.A. from its foundation until his death. During that time, a quarter of a century, there was rarely a meeting, be it of the governing body, the executive committee or subordinate committees that he did not chair. The M.D.A. during this period was a missionary enterprise supporting existing causes and founding numerous new ones. As late as the summer of 1883 he was dedicating new churches in Longsight and Oldham Road and the M.D.A. Annual Report for that year said:

> It has been a source of deep thankfulness to all the members of the Association that their dear and venerated friend the Revd. William Gaskell has been able to dedicate these two new Churches to the Worship and the preaching of that pure and simple Gospel to which he has borne such faithful testimony for more than half a century. None have rejoiced more than he in the completion of a work which is the most important in magnitude the Association has yet undertaken. As Chairman of the Association from its formation in 1859, Mr Gaskell has always given his services most freely to its work: and your committee feels that the Association will gladly seize this opportunity of expressing its deep sense of obligation to him, and also hoping that he may long be spared to encourage all the friends of liberal Christianity in carrying the message of the Gospel of Love of our Heavenly Father to his children.

Mr Head adds this note: 'in a very real sense William Gaskell was the M.D.A. and the M.D.A. was William Gaskell. He was a dedicated Unitarian missionary in the broadest sense - probably the most influential of his generation'.

Bibliography

Unitarian influences

Beard, J.R., ed. *Collection of Hymns for private and public worship*. 1837.

Burney, Lester. *Cross Street Chapel and its College. 1786-1915*. 1983.

Burney, Lester. *Cross Street Chapel Schools. 1734-1942*. 1977.

Carpenter, Joseph Estlin. *James Martineau, theologian and teacher*. 1905.

Christian Life and Unitarian Herald, 6 June 1908 and 10 May 1913.

Davis, V.D. *History of Manchester College* 1932.

Dictionary of National Biography

Drummond, James. *The life and letters of James Martineau*. 1902.

Gaskell, William. (Published sermons and addresses)
(Held in the Unitarian College Collection at John Rylands University Library.)

Gordon, Alexander. *What Manchester owed to Cross Street Chapel*. 1922.

Harris, Paul, ed. *A short history of Rosslyn Hill Chapel. 1692-1973*. 1973.
(An example of the development of a Dissenting meeting place to a recognised Unitarian Church.)

Hill, Andrew. *What do Unitarians Believe?* 1973

McLachlan, H. Cross Street Chapel in the life of Manchester. *Proceedings of the Manchester Literary and Philosophical Society*. 1939-40.

McLachlan, H. *The Unitarian Home Missionary College*. 1915.

McLachlan, H. The Unitarian Movement in the religious life of England. 1934.

The Unitarians (Lindsey Press N.D.)

Personal life

Chadwick, Ellis H. *Mrs Gaskell, haunts, homes and stories*. 1910.

Chapple, J.A.V. *Elizabeth Gaskell, a portrait in letters*. 1981.

Chapple, J.A.V. and Pollard, Arthur, eds.
Letters of Mrs Gaskell. 1966

Easson, Angus. *Elizabeth Gaskell*. 1979.

Gérin, Winifred. *Life of Elizabeth Gaskell*. 1976.

The Lit. & Phil. 1781-1981. Bicentenary booklet, Manchester Literary and Philosophical Society. 1981.

Obituary notices of William Gaskell. In: the *Manchester Guardian*, the *Inquirer*, the *Warrington Guardian* and the *Warrington Examiner*. June 1884.

Payne, George. *Mrs Gaskell and Knutsford*. 2nd ed. 1905.

Sanders, Gerald de Witt. *Elizabeth Gaskell*. 1929.

Shaen, Margaret. *Memorials of two sisters*. 1908.

Chapter 1 Early influences

Aikin, John. *A description of the country from thirty to forty miles round Manchester*. 1795.

Beamont, William. The Reverend Joseph Saul. In: *Warrington Church Notes*. 1878.

Bulmer, J.R., transcriber. *Records of Cairo Street (formerly Sankey Street) Chapel*. 1980.

Carter, George A. *Warrington and the Mid-Mersey Valley*. 1971.

Collins, Herbert Cecil. *Lancashire plain and seaboard*. 1953.

Gooderson, P.J. *History of Lancashire*. 1980.

Gornall, Dr Guest. Study of the life of Samuel Gaskell. Manuscript. (Held in Warrington Library.)

Obituary notice of William Gaskell Senior. in: *Monthly Repository of Theology and general Literature*, 14, 1819.

Palmer, W.T. *The River Mersey*. 1944.

Ramsden, G.M. *A record of the Kay Family of Bury, Lancashire, in the 17th and 18th Centuries*. With notes on the families of Gaskell, Magnall and Darbishire. (1979).

Chapter 2 Preparing for the Ministry

Eminent Unitarian Teachers: & Priestley
(Lindsey Press N.D.)

Evidence given before the University Commissioners of Scotland. 1827.

Murray, David. *Memories of the Old College of Glasgow*. 1927.

Chapter 3 Preacher at Cross Street Chapel

Evans, John. *Lancashire authors and orators*. 1850.

Harland, John. Annals: 1806-1868.

Manuscript.

Wright, J.J. *Young days*. 1899.

Extract quoted in: Payne, George. *Mrs Gaskell and Knutsford*. 2nd ed. 1905.

Chapter 4 Husband and Father

Chapple, J.A.V. An author's life; Elizabeth Gaskell and the Wedgwood family. *Transactions of the Brontë Society*. June 1979.

Gaskell, Elizabeth (Cotton Mills Mather Esq)
Life in Manchester (1847): *Libby Marsh's three eras*.
Facsimile reprint from Howitt's Journal 1847 published by Lancashire and Cheshire Antiquarian Society. 1968.

Gaskell, Elizabeth. *My diary: the early years of my daughter Marianne*. 1923. Limited edition of fifty copies privately printed by C.K. Shorter for presentation only.
(Held in the Gaskell Collection, Manchester Central Library.)

Newspaper cuttings in the Gaskell file at the Headquarters of the International Society, 84 Plymouth Grove.

Chapter 5 Literary Interests

Gaskell, Elizabeth. *Mary Barton*. 1848.

(Gaskell, Elizabeth and Gaskell, William.) Sketches among the poor No. 1. *Blackwood's Edinburgh Magazines*, 41, 1837, p.48-50.

Gaskell, William. *Two lectures on the Lancashire dialect.* 1854.
Glendinning, Sheran Elizabeth. Christian ideology and *Mary Barton,* influences of Unitarianism. (BA (Hons.) degree dissertation). (Held in Cross Street Chapel archives.)
Reports of the Ministry to the Poor from 1833. (Held in Cross Street Chapel archives.)
Reports on Manchester Domestic Mission. (Held in Cross Street Chapel archives.)

Chapter 6 As Teacher—preparing the way
Gaskell, William. *Discourse to Manchester and District Sunday Schools at Bank Street Chapel, Bolton on Good Friday, 29 March 1850.* (Held in the Unitarian College Collection at John Rylands University Library.)

Chapter 7 As Teacher—spreading the word
Adams, W.E. *Memoirs of a social atom.* 1903. 2 vols.
Beard, John Relly and Gaskell, William. *The address delivered at the inaugural meeting of the Unitarian Home Missionary Board,* at Cross Street Chapel, on 4 December 1854. 1855.
Davies, C. Stella. *History of Macclesfield.* 1961.
Gaskell, William. *Address at the inaugural meeting of the Unitarian Home Missionary Board at Cross Street Chapel, on December 4th 1854.*
Green, Roger Lancelyn. *Mrs Molesworth.* 1961.
Molesworth, Mrs M.L. *The carved lions.* 1895.
Rushton, Adam. *My life as farmer's boy, factory hand, teacher and preacher.* 1909.
Winkworth, Catherine, transl. *Lyra Germanica: the Christian life.* 1855.

Chapter 8 The crowded days at Plymouth Grove
Gaskell, Elizabeth. *Cousin Phillis and other tales.* 1865.
Gaskell, Elizabeth. *North and South.* 1855.
Gaskell, Elizabeth. *Ruth.* 1853.
Gaskell, Elizabeth. *Sylvia's lovers.* 1863.
Gaskell, Elizabeth. *Wives and daughters.* 1866.
Gérin, Winifred. *Life of Charlotte Brontë.* 1976.
Nicholson, Helen M. A brief account of the life and ministry of William Turner. *Transactions of the Unitarian Historical Society.* April. 1983.

Chapter 9 The Last Years
Cross Street Chapel, Manchester, 1878. Commemoration of the Rev. William Gaskell's Fifty Years' Ministry. 15 October 1878. (Held in the Unitarian College Collection at the John Rylands University Library.
Drummond, James. *The holiness of human sorrow:* a sermon preached at Cross Street Chapel, Manchester, on 19 November 1865, on the occasion of the sudden death of Mrs Gaskell. 1865.

(Held in the Unitarian College Collection at John Rylands University Library.)

Gaskell, William. (Manuscript letters)
(Held in the Unitarian College Collection at John Rylands University Library.)

Gaskell, William.
(Newspaper report of a lecture given by William Gaskell on Crabbe and his poetry.) in: *The Manchester Guardian* 9 March 1872.

Gaskell, William. *The strong points of Unitarian Christianity*. Lecture given at the bicentenary commemoration service at Mill Hill Chapel, Leeds, on 30 October 1873.
(Held in the Unitarian College Collection at John Rylands University Library.)

Gaskell, William. *Submission to the will of God:* a sermon preached on the occasion the death of Mrs Gallenga, preached at Cross Street Chapel, on 30 September 1855. 1855.
(Held in the Unitarian College Collection at John Rylands University Library.)

Manchester and Salford Sanitary Association. *Annual reports.* 1853-1880.
(Held in Manchester Central Library.)

Minutes of the Provincial Assembly of Presbyterian and Unitarian Ministers 1822-4.
(Held in the Unitarian College Collection at the John Rylands University Library)

Potter, Beatrix. *Journal: 1881-1897.* Transcribed by Leslie Linder. 1966.

Chapter 10 A century on

Farjeon, Eleanor. *Edward Thomas, the last four years. Memoirs. Book 1.* 1958.

Manchester College, Oxford. *Annual Report, 1982.*

Newspaper cuttings about the Gaskells and correspondence about the purchase of 84 Plymouth Grove for the International Society.
(Held at 84 Plymouth Grove.)

Newspaper cuttings on the Misses Gaskell, including obituary notices.
(Held in the Gaskell Collection, Manchester Central Library.)

Pape, T. 'Silverdale Literary and Historical' *Morecambe Visitor.* 1911.

Portico Library, Manchester. Minute books. Manuscript.

Thomas, Edward. The Sheiling. In: Thomas, R. George, ed. *The collected poems of Edward Thomas.* 1978.

Unitarian College, Manchester. *Annual Report, 1982.*

Wilson, A. Vincent. *A short history of Cross Street Chapel's Wayside Pulpit.* 1970.

Index

INDEX

WILLIAM GASKELL

S A L F O R D

PEEL PARK

Goods Yard

MAP OF

MANCHESTER

Scale

Divided into ½ Mile Squares and Circles,

Railway & Stations